W9-CQJ-101

Lynn Andersen

Modern Danish Cooking

NYT NORDISK FORLAG ARNOLD BUSCK

Contents

Modern Danish Cooking

The Danes are leading a culinary revolution. Copenhagen is one the most influential food cities in the world, because of the much talked about food from the North.

That is not, however, how I experienced Denmark when I pulled in at the Copenhagen train station as a poor student many years ago. My plan was to spend a year in Denmark studying at the University and after that time, I was to spend another six months travelling around Europe. I was forced to eat as cheaply as possible, and when I did get some money, I wasted it on expensive and inferior products imported from far-off places. I longed for the food that I was used too. I missed the California sunshine and its many delightful vegetables and fruit.

Tired of eating at the cheapest cafeterias in Copenhagen, freezing for lack of proper clothing, no money to spare, I called home – collect. It started to snow, the snowflakes spattering onto the window of the phone box only to vanish immediately. It was November, I was miserable, and I had only been in Copenhagen a few months. My family immediately urged me to come home. They even offered to pay my plane ticket back to sunny California.

I refused their offer and was determined to make the best of my time in Denmark. Hurrying over the snow covered ground; I made up my mind to give the Danish kitchen a chance. I had met a Dane, and something told me I would be sticking around a lot longer than a year and a half. I enrolled at the teacher training college (Suhrs Seminarium) where I learned to cook and began to appreciate the Danish way of cooking.

The Danes, like all nationalities, have their traditions and their customs. Who hasn't heard of "Danish" pastry and Danish open-face sandwiches? In spite of a long tradition of Danish cooking, the Danes, like so many other countries, had suddenly discovered other cuisines when they began to travel in the beginning of the 1960's. At first they took short trips around Europe and later they journeyed as far as the United States. They moved on to Asia, Australia, New Zealand and South America. They also adopted traditions, food and customs of other countries, pushing the Danish products aside. By the 1980's, there was little or no interest for local products.

Thank goodness, this has changed over the past few years, and the Danish people are rebelling against the blandness of food created over hundreds of years of puritanical eating habits. They are also rebelling against the latest in mega-farming Agro efficiencies as well as the society's concepts that only notable foods from Europe's culinary Meccas merited the attention of smart local foodies. Olive oil, Iberico Ham, Truffles, and Foie Gras were all the rage and had nothing to do with local Danish products. People started asking themselves, "Could these be the only foods worthy of eating?"

The Danes are now saying, "Use only local ingredients. We have such rich and diverse foods to choose from. We ask ourselves why go elsewhere? Use seasonal ingredients. We can live better and in harmony with nature. Prepare healthy foods rich in grains, fish, fruit and vegetables – without being bland. Good food is meant to delight and give pleasure."

Now it is time to begin exploring a few new ideas, based on many of the same principles of the New Nordic Kitchen and share with others the food that I have been eating and enjoying for the past forty years.

I for one am quite fond of the Danish kitchen and hope that you will enjoy it as much as I have enjoyed writing this book.

You may have trouble finding exactly the same ingredients in the recipes, but in most cases, you can find appropriate substitutes in your area.

Lynn Andersen

Metric Conversion Chart

Temperature equivalents

Fahrenheit		Celsius
0°	(freezer temperature)	-18°
32°	(water freezes)	0°
98.6°		37°
180°	(water simmers)	82°
212°	(water boils)	100°
250°	(low oven)	120°
350°	(moderate oven)	175°
425°	(hot oven)	220°
500°	(very hot oven)	260°

Conversion formula: Degrees Fahrenheit minus 32 divided by 1.8 = degrees Celsius

Weight Equivalents
(ounces and pounds/grams and kilograms)

US	Metric
¼ oz.	7 g
½ oz.	15 g
¾ oz.	20 g
1 oz.	30 g
8 oz. (½ lb)	225 g
12 oz. (¾ lb)	340 g
16 oz. (1 lb)	455 g
35 oz. (2.2 lb)	1 kg

Conversion formula: Ounces x 28.25 = grams
1000 grams = 1 kilograms

Volume Equivalents
(fluid ounces/milliliters and liters)

US	Metric
1 tsp.	5 ml
1 tbsp (½ fl. oz.)	15 ml
¼ cup (2 fl. oz.)	60 ml
⅓ cup	80 ml
½ cup (fl. oz.)	120 ml
¾ cup (6 fl. oz.)	160 ml
1 cup (8 fl. oz.)	240 ml
1 qt. (32 fl. oz.)	950 ml
1 qt. + 3 tbsp.	1 L
1 gal. (128 fl oz.)	4 L

Conversion formula: Fluid ounces x 30 = milliliters
1000 milliliters = 1 liter

Measurements
4 tbsp. = ¼ cup = ½ dl
6 tbsp. ⅓ cup
1 stick (of butter) 8 tbsp. = ½ cup = 1 dl

Where to buy special ingredients

www.bobsredmill.com rye flour and other sorts of grain for baking

www.wholefoodsmarket.com organic health food stores with products from all over the world, including rye flour, danish cheese, fresh and canned caviar

www.traderjoes.com large selection of products from all over the world

www.ikea.com have some Scandinavien products (mostly from Sweden)

Try local farmers markets for fresh local produce and health food stores

P22. 60 Pass.

Spring

Asparagus with Poached Eggs

4 appetizer servings

16 spears green asparagus, trimmed
salt to taste
8 slices of bacon
4 oz. butter
1 8 oz. bunch fresh parsley or a mixture of several herbs
7 tbsp. butter, room temperature
½ tsp. lemon zest
salt

Poached eggs:
4 large eggs
water, salt

Garnish:
1 spear raw asparagus
pea tendrils*

To make asparagus, place asparagus in salted boiling water and cook until just tender but still bright green. Remove from the boiling water and plunge them into ice water to stop the cooking process. Drain and set aside.

To make the bacon, cook bacon in a large skillet over medium heat until crisp. Transfer bacon to paper towels to drain.

To make the parsley butter, combine lemon zest, herbs, salt and softened butter on a cutting board. Using a large knife, finely chop all ingredients together until well combined. Place in a small bowl.

To make the eggs, bring a large skillet of water just to simmer over medium-low heat. Sprinkle water with salt. Working with 1 egg at a time, crack egg into a cup and slide egg into simmering water. Cook eggs until whites are cooked through but yolks are still runny, 3-4 minutes. Using a slotted spoon, transfer poached eggs to medium bowl filled with ice water to stop cooking.

To serve, arrange asparagus on 4 plates, sprinkle crumbled bacon over and place a poached egg on top. Place a spoonful of herb butter on the asparagus. Using a potato peeler, cut strips of raw asparagus and garnish the dish with them and pea tendrils.

* Pea tendrils, the shoots and leaves that appear on top of new pea plants in the early spring, are tender little greens that taste like a cross between peas and spinach.

Open-face Sandwich with Roast Beef, Spicy Remoulade and Cucumber Salad

8 appetizer servings

Spicy remoulade:
½ cup mayonnaise
3 tbsp. prepared horseradish
2 tbsp. ramsons or 2 tbsp. chopped scallions
1 tsp. freshly squeezed lemon juice
kosher salt and freshly ground pepper

8 small slices rye bread (see page 33)
2 oz. butter (optional)
16 slices of rare roast beef

Cucumber salad: (see page 57)
1 tbsp. chopped parsley

To make the remoulade, whisk the first 4 ingredients in a small bowl. Season with salt and pepper. Set aside.
To make the sandwich, spread rye bread with butter if using. Arrange 2 slices roast beef on bread and place a spoonful on one side of the sandwich (a little off center) and a spoonful of cucumber salad next to remoulade. Do not place on top of remoulade as it will quickly become soggy. Sprinkle with parsley.

Danish open-face sandwiches are one of the most prominent features of the Danish kitchen. A slice of rye bread or a slice of white bread with a little butter, and you can make all kinds of interesting sandwiches. Here are a few suggestions; fish cakes page 48 sliced with a spoonful remoulade, tartare made as described in the recipe on page 99 placed on dark rye bread page 33. Spice-Cured Veal with Pear salad, page 91 would also be nice on dark bread.

Salmon Tartare with Parsley Oil and White Asparagus

4 appetizer servings

8 peeled white asparagus
Parsley oil:
5 oz. parsley
½ cup corn oil
1-2 tbsp. apple cider vinegar
salt and freshly ground pepper
Salmon tartare:
6-8 oz. fresh salmon without skin, cut into ¼ inch dice
2 tbsp. lemon juice
2 tbsp. rapeseed oil
2 tbsp. capers

Garnish:
cress

To make the asparagus, cook asparagus in salted water. Cook 4-6 minutes depending on how thick they are. Remove them from the boiling water and plunge them into ice water to stop the cooking process. As soon as they are cool, transfer them to 4 plates and set aside.

To make the parsley oil, place all ingredients in a food processor and blend until smooth.

To make the tartare, combine all the ingredients for salmon tartare in a bowl. Do not make the tartare before the last minute as the acid in the lemon juice will 'cook' the fish, turning it opaque and milky-colored.

To serve, divide salmon into 4 portions and press salmon tartare into a ring in order to form the tartare. If you don't have a ring to form the tartare, place the tartare attractively on 4 plates and arrange 2 spears of asparagus on each plate. With a small spoon, drizzle parsley oil around the plate. Garnish with cress.

Spring Salad with Shrimps and Peas

4 salad servings

Marinade:
4 tbsp. rapeseed oil
1 tbsp. apple cider vinegar
6-7 oz. cooked shrimps
5-6 oz. fresh, shelled peas, cooked 1-2 minutes
2 tbsp. finely chopped dill
6-7 oz. baby shrimps
1 head Bibb lettuce

Horseradish dressing:
1 cup homemade mayonnaise or 1 cup good mayonnaise
3-4 tbsp. sour cream
2 tbsp. grated horseradish

Garnish:
4 sprigs dill
pea tendrils*

To make the salad, whisk vinegar and oil together in a bowl and add shrimps, peas and dill. Set aside.
To make the horseradish dressing, whisk mayonnaise, sour cream and horseradish in a small bowl.
To serve, place 2-3 lettuce leaves on 4 plates. Place a mound of shrimp salad on each plate. Spoon a tablespoon of horseradish dressing on top of each mound of shrimp salad and garnish with dill. Serve remaining dressing on the side.

To make the mayonnaise, take all the ingredients out of the refrigerator an hour before making the mayonnaise. If you use rapeseed oil, the mayonnaise will be a beautiful yellow color.

Makes 2 cups
2 fresh yolks or 1 whole egg**
4 tsp. vinegar
1 tbsp. Dijon mustard
¼ tsp. salt
1 pinch of freshly ground white pepper
1 tbsp. freshly squeezed lemon juice
1 cup of corn/rapeseed oil

Combine the egg yolks/whites, vinegar, mustard, salt, white pepper and lemon juice. Process until blended. With the machine running, slowly add the oil in a thin stream and process until emulsified.

* Pea tendrils, the shoots and leaves that appear on top of new pea plants in the early spring, are tender little greens that taste like a cross between peas and spinach.

** Mayonnaise can be made with both yolks and whites of an egg. It will be lighter and not quite so rich in taste.

Asparagus with Morel Cream and Crisp Chicken Skin

4 appetizers or lunch servings

Skin from a chicken, not necessarily in one piece
coarse salt
16 spears green and white asparagus, trimmed
2 heads butter lettuce
12 fresh chervil sprigs
3 oz. fresh morel mushrooms or 1 oz. dried, finely chopped
5 tbsp. heavy cream
juice of ½ lemon
freshly ground black pepper

Preheat oven to 400° F.
To make the chicken skin, trim chicken skin for excess fat and cut into smaller pieces which can lay flat. Place a sheet of parchment paper on a baking sheet pan and place chicken skins on top of paper. Sprinkle with coarse salt. Place another sheet of parchment paper over and set another baking sheet pan over. This will keep chicken skin from curling. Bake 15 minutes. Transfer skin to a flat tray. Let cool completely before breaking them into smaller pieces.
To make the salad, cut asparagus in thin slices with a potato peeler or a mandolin. Rinse lettuce and chervil sprigs and tear into smaller pieces. Mix morel mushrooms with cream and lemon juice for a dressing. Season with salt and pepper and pour over the asparagus, salad and chervil sprigs.
To serve, divide salad on 4 plates. Sprinkle with chicken skins and black pepper.

Suggested accompaniment: add cooked chicken slices to the salad for a more filling lunch dish.

Salad with Grandmother's Dressing

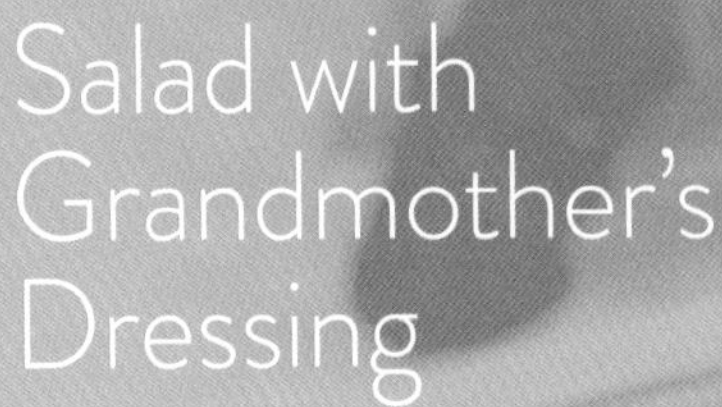

4 salad servings

Dressing:
½ cup heavy cream
juice of a lemon
2 tbsp. sugar
salt and freshly ground pepper

2 heads Bibb lettuce/butter lettuce
1 cup mixed herbs such as flat-leaf parsley, sorrel, dill and flowers
zest of lemon
blueberries or another fresh berry

To make the dressing, whisk cream, lemon juice and sugar in a bowl to blend. Season with salt and pepper.
To serve, arrange lettuce and herbs nicely on serving platter; spoon dressing over and garnish with zest of lemon and blueberries.

In keeping with the New Nordic Kitchen, Danes are returning to old classic recipes like this one. Danish grandmothers knew nothing about oils and vinegar dressing and often used heavy cream as dressing.

Lemon Marinated Salmon with Horseradish Dressing

12 appetizer servings

3 lbs. salmon fillet, with skin left on

Marinade:
6 lemons
salt and freshly ground white pepper

Dressing:
1 cup sour cream
2 cups whipped heavy cream
2 tbsp. lemon juice
salt and freshly ground white pepper
2 tbsp. freshly grated horseradish

Garnish:
cress, parsley or chives
4 lemons (optional)

To make the salmon, remove all bones from salmon and place salmon skin side down in a deep dish. Grate rind of 2 lemons and sprinkle over salmon. Squeeze juice from all 6 lemons; pour over salmon. Sprinkle with salt and pepper. Cover and refrigerate for at least 4 hours or overnight. Make sure salmon is covered with juice or turn fillet once or twice while marinating.
To make the horseradish dressing, whisk all ingredients for dressing in a bowl.
To serve, cut salmon in very thin slices diagonally across grain. Cut the 4 lemons in very thin slices and place them in a large circle on a large platter. Place slices of salmon in the middle of the circle and garnish with herbs. Serve dressing on the side.

Warm New Potatoes and Radishes with Lemon-Herb Butter

→

4 lunch or salad servings

1 8 oz. bunch fresh parsley or a mixture of several herbs, divided
7 tbsp. butter, room temperature
½ tsp. lemon zest plus ¼ cup fresh lemon juice
salt and freshly ground pepper
1½ lb. small new potatoes, scrubbed
1 small bunch radishes, trimmed of all but ½ inch of green tops, quartered if large, leaves coarsely torn
4 tbsp. chilled lumpfish, paddlefish or hackleback roe

To make the herb butter, chop leaves from half of herbs; reserve stems. Combine lemon zest, herbs, salt and softened butter on a cutting board. Using a large knife, finely chop all ingredients together until well combined. Place in a small bowl; stir in lemon juice and set aside.
To make the potatoes, cook potatoes and remaining herbs with stems, in a large saucepan of boiling water until just tender, about 10 minutes. Remove from heat and let stand 5 minutes for herbs to infuse.
To serve, drain potatoes. Arrange on a platter. Using the back of a spoon, smash each potato. Dot potatoes generously with lemon-herb butter. Arrange radishes and radish leaves over. Spoon small dollops of roe over and sprinkle lemon juice over. Season with salt and pepper.

Suggested accompaniment: dark rye bread, toasted. See page 33.

Spicy Carrot-Apple Soup with Fresh Mint

6 soup servings

2 tbsp. duck fat or rapeseed oil
1 large finely chopped onion
1½ lb. carrots, peeled, diced, plus 1 carrot peeled, halved lengthwise
3 cups chicken broth
1 large apple or two small, finely diced
2 tsp. chopped fresh ginger
1 cup fresh, pressed apple juice
¼ tsp. freshly grated nutmeg
¼ tsp. ground allspice
kosher salt

Garnish:
chopped fresh mint

To make the soup, heat duck fat in a large saucepan over medium-high heat. Add onion; sauté 2 minutes. Add all the carrots, broth, ¾ of the diced apple and ginger; bring to a boil. Cover. Reduce heat; simmer until carrots are tender, about 20 minutes. Remove carrot halves; dice finely. Puree soup in batches in food processor; return to pan. Mix in apple juice and spices. Season with salt and pepper.
To serve, ladle soup into 4 warmed bowls. Top with finely diced carrot, finely diced apple and mint.

Potato Soup with Ramsons*

4 soup servings

2 tbsp. unsalted butter
1 cup thinly sliced trimmed ramsons*, (stems and green tops) or 1 cup sliced leek and 1 chopped garlic clove
1 lb. russet potatoes, peeled and sliced ¼ inch thick
salt and freshly ground white pepper to taste
3 cups chicken stock
1 cup heavy cream

Garnish:
5-6 ramson leaves, chopped

To make the soup, melt butter in a large saucepan over medium heat; add ramsons and sauté until soft. Add potato and sauté, 2-3 minutes. Season with salt and pepper and add chicken stock. Bring to a boil. Lower heat to simmer and cook until potatoes are very soft, about 20 minutes. Add cream and bring to a boil. Puree in a blender until smooth. Return soup to pan. Taste and adjust seasoning. Cover to keep warm.
To serve, pour soup into 4 warmed bowls. Sprinkle with chopped ramson leaves.

* Ramsons (also known as wild garlic) have garlicky, green flavor that turns mellow with cooking.

→

Sautéed Plaice with Shrimps, Asparagus, and Danish Caviar

4 main course servings

8 large fillets of plaice with the skins removed
4-6 tbsp. dried bread crumbs/flour
2 eggs (if using dried bread crumbs)
salt and freshly ground white pepper
2 oz. butter
1 cup fish stock
½ cup white wine
1 tbsp. butter
½ tbsp. flour
8 oz. freshly shelled shrimps
8 oz. freshly cooked asparagus
1 jar of Danish lumpfish roe or salmon roe

Garnish:
4 sprigs of chervil

To make the fish, rinse, pat dry and dredge fish fillets in a mixture of flour, salt and pepper. If using bread crumbs, whip eggs with a fork and coat fish fillets first in egg mixture and then coat them with bread crumbs. Melt butter in a large frying pan and fry two fillets at a time over medium heat 1-2 minutes. Turn them and fry them 1-2 minutes. Repeat this process with the next two fish fillets. Place them on a warm serving dish. Cover and keep warm.

To make the sauce, boil fish stock rapidly until it is reduced to half; add white wine. Blend butter and flour to make a smooth paste. Whisk butter/flour mixture into stock and bring to a boil. Reduce heat to low and simmer 3-4 minutes. Season with salt and pepper.

To serve, place two sautéed fillets on each warmed plate. Drizzle sauce on the fillets. Place a fourth of the shrimps on each fish fillet and 1-2 spears of asparagus on top of the shrimps. Place a generous tablespoon of lumpfish/salmon roe next to the asparagus spears. Garnish with chervil. Pass remaining sauce to the fish.

Suggested accompaniment: new baby potatoes.

Crème Barley with Salsify and Salmon

4 main course servings

Barley with salsify:
20 salsify roots, scrubbed and trimmed
2 tbsp. rapeseed oil
3 finely chopped shallots
2 cups barley
1 cup dry white wine
1 quart water
salt and freshly ground pepper
3 oz. havarti cheese
juice of a lemon
½ bunch of chopped fresh thyme
½ bunch of chopped parsley

Salmon:
4 6 oz. salmon steaks, each ¾ inch thick
4 tbsp. butter
zest and juice of a lemon

Garnish:
chervil sprigs

Preheat oven to 325°F.
To make the barley, heat oil in a pot and sauté shallots 1 minute over medium heat. Chop 4 salsify roots coarsely and add them to pot and sauté 1 minute. Add barley and sauté 1 minute. Add wine and cook until liquid is gone. Add water and let barley simmer 30 minutes without covering. Add lemon juice.
Shred cheese and add to barley with thyme and parsley. Season with salt and pepper.
To make the salmon, place salmon steaks in a dish, sprinkle with zest and juice of a lemon. Place butter on top of salmon steaks and set in warm oven, about 20-25 minutes.
To make the salsify, blanch remaining roots of salsify 2-4 minutes. depending on thickness in salted boiling water.
To serve, place 4 salsify in center of 4 warmed plates, mound barley over and top with a salmon steak. Garnish with chervil sprigs.

Lamb Chops with Rhubarb Chutney

4 main course servings

Chutney:
1 finely chopped onion
8 oz. rhubarb, cleaned and diced
4 tbsp. sugar
½ cup apple cider vinegar

Lamb chops:
8-12 lamb chops, frenched
oil for the grill
salt and freshly ground pepper

Garnish:
pea tendrils* or parsley

To make the chutney, place onion, rhubarb, sugar and vinegar in a saucepan and bring to a boil, stirring until sugar has dissolved. Reduce heat and simmer for about 6-8 minutes. Remove saucepan from stove and let chutney cool for 5 minutes. It is important not to overcook the rhubarb.
Prepare a fire in a charcoal grill or preheat a gas grill.
To make the lamb chops, season lamp chops with salt. Grill lightly on both sides until well marked but still moist inside. Alternatively, broil for 8 min.
To serve, divide lamb chops on 4 warmed plates and mound chutney next to lamb chops. Garnish with pea tendrils or parsley.

Suggested accompaniment: smoked new baby potatoes (see page 52) and spring vegetables.

* The shoots and leaves that appear on the top of new pea plants in the early spring are tender little greens that taste like a cross between peas and spinach.

Ragout of Morel Mushrooms and Asparagus with Red Fish

6 main course servings

Ragout:
2 tbsp. butter
1 large leek, trimmed, split and washed thoroughly to remove grit, and sliced
4 small new carrots, trimmed and whole if very small, or cut in halves
1 small sliced onion
3 oz. morel mushrooms, cleaned and halved if they are large
2 tbsp. vegetable stock
1 cup heavy cream
6 large white asparagus, peeled or 8 small green, trimmed, blanched for 6-8 minutes for white and 2-4 minutes for green

Redfish (ocean perch):
6 redfish fillets with skin, scales removed
2-3 tbsp. rapeseed oil

Garnish:
½ tsp. coarse sea salt
2 tbsp. finely chopped chives

To make the ragout, melt butter in a medium saucepan over medium heat and sauté leek, carrot and onion until soft, about 2 minutes. Add morels and sauté for 1 minute. Add stock and cream and bring to a boil. Set aside and keep warm. Just before serving, add asparagus and heat for 2 minutes.

To sauté redfish, warm oil in a medium skillet over medium heat and place fish, skin side down. Place a little plate over fish in order to keep it flat. The fish should not be sautéed on the other side.

To serve, divide ragout among 6 warmed plates. Place a fillet, skin side up, on top of the ragout. Sprinkle with salt and chives.

Sautéed Chicken and Radishes with Mustard and Ramsons*

4 main course servings

4 skinless boneless chicken breasts
kosher salt and freshly ground pepper
3 tbsp. butter, divided
2 tbsp. rapeseed oil, divided
2 tbsp. minced shallot
¼ cup dry white wine
1 cup chicken stock
1 tbsp. Dijon mustard
2 tbsp. chopped ramsons or spring onions
2 bunches radishes, trimmed of all but ½ inch of green tops, radishes halved lengthwise

Garnish:
chopped ramsons* or spring onions

To make the chicken, sprinkle chicken with salt and pepper. Melt 1 tbsp. butter with 1 tablespoon oil in a large skillet over medium-high heat and cook until browned and cooked through, 5-6 minutes per side, depending on thickness. Transfer chicken to plate; cover to keep warm. Add shallot to same skillet; stir over medium-high heat 1 minute. Add wine, then stock to skillet; bring to a boil. Whisk in mustard and chopped ramsons; boil until sauce thickens enough to coat spoon and is reduced to ½ cup, 5-6 minutes. Stir in 1 tbsp. butter; set aside.
To make the radishes, melt remaining butter with remaining oil in heavy skillet over medium-high heat. Add radishes; sprinkle with salt and pepper; cook without stirring until radishes begin to brown, about 4 minutes.
To serve, cut chicken breasts crosswise and divide among 4 warmed plates. Place radishes around and over chicken. Spoon sauce over chicken and radishes. Garnish with ramsons or spring onions.

Suggested accompaniment: crème barley (see page 21).

Brief, high heat roasting mellows a radish's peppery flavor and turns it into a whole new root vegetable. Using the green tops adds color and enhances the radish flavor.

* Ramsons (also known as wild garlic) have garlicky, green flavor that turns mellow with cooking.

Lamb Fricassee with Spring Vegetables

6-8 main course servings

3 lb. bone-in-lamb shoulder
3 tsp. salt per quart of water

Bouquet garni:
1 leek top (only the green leaves)
2 sprigs of thyme
1 bay leaf
2 sprigs of parsley
String to tie bouquet garni
1½ lb. new carrots, leave them whole if they are small, if not, slice into 1½ inch pieces
1 lb. green asparagus, trimmed and cut into 1½ inch pieces
2 cups light cream
5 tbsp. cornstarch
5-6 oz. fresh, shelled peas
salt and freshly ground pepper

Garnish:
1 bunch dill

To make the lamb, put meat in a pot and pour enough water to just cover. Bring to a boil and skim the broth. Add salt and bouquet garni to pot. Cover and simmer over low heat, about 1½ hours.
To make the vegetables, transfer meat to a plate and remove bones. Cut or shred meat into bite-size pieces and set aside. Remove bouquet garni and cook carrots and asparagus 2-3 minutes in cooking liquid. Transfer vegetables to a plate and strain 1 quart of liquid into a large pot. Stir cornstarch into cream and pour into pot with cooking broth. Boil broth 2 minutes. Add carrots, asparagus and peas and bring to boil. Add meat, season with salt and pepper.
To serve, divide fricassee among 8 warmed plates and sprinkle with dill.

Suggested accompaniment: boiled new potatoes.

Scallops with Pickled Onions, Steamed Leeks and Crisp Onions

6 appetizer servings

Pickled onions:
6 small shallots
1 tsp. salt
½ cup apple cider vinegar
2 tbsp. sugar

Crisp onions:
2 medium onions, minced
1 tbsp. flour
2 tbsp. rapeseed oil

Steamed leeks:
3 small leeks, trimmed and washed thoroughly to remove grit, cut into 4 inch pieces
2 tbsp. butter
2 tbsp. water

Scallops:
1½ tbsp. rapeseed oil or vegetable oil
12 large sea scallops, side muscle removed
kosher salt
freshly ground black pepper

Parsley oil:
1 cup flat-leaf parsley leaves, finely chopped
3-4 tbsp. rapeseed oil

Garnish:
cress

To make the pickled shallots, cut shallots into 4 sections and place in a medium bowl. Sprinkle with salt and set aside for 30 minutes. Whisk together vinegar and sugar. Add shallots, toss well. Marinate in refrigerator for 1 hour.
To make the fried onions, dust minced onions with flour. Heat oil in a medium pan and fry until they are golden and crisp.
To make the leeks, melt butter in a medium skillet over low heat. Add water and leeks sauté 10-15 minutes. Add more water if needed while cooking.
To make the parsley oil, blend parsley and oil.
To make the scallops, heat oil in a large heavy skillet over high heat until oil begins to smoke. Season scallops with salt and pepper. Sear until well browned, about 2 minutes. Turn; cook until just barely opaque in center, about 30 seconds longer.
To serve, place two spoonfuls of parsley oil on 6 plates and place one leek, two scallops and a spoonful of pickled onions on top of the oil. Garnish with crisp onions and cress.

Rhubarb Compote with Yoghurt and Oat Hazelnut Crunch

4 dessert servings

10 oz. rhubarb, trimmed, cut into 2 inch-long pieces
4 oz. sugar, divided
½ vanilla bean, split lengthwise
1 cup oats
2 oz. chopped hazelnuts
10 oz. Greek yoghurt

To make the compote, place rhubarb and 2 oz. of sugar in a pot with 2 tbsp. water. Scrape seeds from vanilla bean and add to pot along with bean. Bring just to a boil and simmer 5 minutes. Remove bean and set aside.
To make the crunch, melt the remaining sugar in a small pan and stir in oats and hazelnuts. Set aside and let the crunch cool completely.
To serve, divide compote into 4 glasses and place a large dollop of yoghurt on top. Sprinkle the crunch over the yoghurt.

Chilled Rhubarb Soup with Mint

→

6 dessert servings

1½ lb. rhubarb, trimmed, cut into 1 inch pieces
2 vanilla beans split lengthwise
1½ quart water
1½ cup sugar

Garnish:
mint leaves
sour cream

To make the soup, place rhubarb in a large pot. Scrape seeds from vanilla bean and add them to pot along with bean and water. Bring to a boil; reduce heat to low and simmer, covered, 30 minutes.
Remove bean, strain through a fine-mesh sieve into a clean pot, and add sugar. Bring to a boil and stir until sugar is dissolved. Pour soup into a large bowl to cool, then cover and refrigerate overnight.
To serve, pour soup into 6 chilled soup bowls, add a spoonful sour cream or whipped cream to each bowl, garnish with mint.

Danish Dark Rye Bread

Sourdough starter:
1 cup plain yoghurt
½ oz. approx. (one package) of active dry yeast
1½ cup rye flour
1 tsp. salt

Dough:
sourdough starter
1½ pint water
1¾ lb. rye flour
1 tbsp. salt
melted butter

To make the sourdough starter, combine yoghurt, dry yeast, flour and salt in a bowl. Cover bowl with plastic wrap and place in refrigerator for three days until dough begins to bubble.

To make the rye bread, dilute sourdough starter with water. Add rye flour and salt. Cover with a dish towel and let dough rest in a warm place until the next day.

The next day, turn dough onto a lightly floured surface and knead until smooth. Remove approx. 1 cup dough as a starter for the next bread. Put it in a clean container, cover with plastic wrap and place it in the refrigerator.*

To bake the bread, brush a 2 quart loaf tin with melted butter. Place dough in the tin, cover with a clean dish towel and let rise 4 hours in a warm place. Place bread in a cold oven. Set the temperature to 350°F and bake for 1½ to 2 hours.

Wrap bread in a clean dish towel and cool on a baking rack. It is best not to cut the bread until the next day.

* Always take a lump of dough each time you make this bread and put it in the refrigerator. This way you will always have a starter for the next bread you make. The starter will stay fresh for 3 weeks. It can be frozen for up to 3 months. Be sure to take it out one or two days ahead of time and thaw it up in the refrigerator. After the starter is thawed, it should be left at least one day before being used.

Danish rye bread (rugbrød) is a very important part of the Danish diet. Many of the Danish open-face sandwiches call for dark bread, rugbrød. It can also be sliced thinly and toasted in the oven and served as an accompaniment to salad, soups and stews. One of the most popular Danish dishes is bread and beer porridge, called øllebrød in Danish. It is made with dried rugbrød (Danish rye bread) and the recipe can be found on page 115.

O54
H 14
333

Summer

Shrimps with Two Sauces

4 appetizer servings

3-4 lbs. cooked shrimps with their shell

Garlic mayonnaise with ramsons*:
2 fresh yolks or 1 whole egg**
4 tsp. apple cider vinegar
¼ tsp. salt
a pinch of freshly ground white pepper
1 tbsp. freshly squeezed lemon juice
1 cup of rapeseed/corn oil
1 cup thinly sliced trimmed ramsons (stems, and green tops) or ½ cup sliced spring onions and 1 minced garlic clove

Dill sour cream:
1 cup sour cream
2 tsp. minced shallot
1 tsp. chopped fresh dill
1 tsp. freshly squeezed lemon juice
salt and freshly ground white pepper to taste
1-2 lemons, cut into wedges

* Ramsons are wild garlic plants that grow in fields but also in parks and gardens. They both smell and taste of garlic. They can be eaten raw or cooked.

** Mayonnaise can be made with both yolks and whites of an egg. It will be lighter and not quite so rich in taste.

To serve, place a large bowl on the table with shrimps and let the guests shell their own shrimps. To shell the shrimps, pull off head and legs. Starting with the head end, pull off outer shell. The last segment of the shell and tail tip can be left on for decorative purposes.
Serve with one or two dips and slices of lemon.
To make the garlic mayonnaise, all ingredients should have room temperature. Combine egg yolks/whites, vinegar, salt, white pepper and lemon juice in a food processor. Process until blended. With the machine running, slowly add oil in a thin stream and process until emulsified. Stir ramsons/onions and garlic in.
To make the dill sour cream, whisk together sour cream, shallot, dill and lemon juice in a small bowl. Season with salt and pepper. Cover and refrigerate until the dip should be served.

Smoked Salmon and Shrimp Open-face Sandwich

8 appetizer servings

3 tbsp. butter at room temperature
1 tbsp. prepared horseradish
1 tbsp. sour cream
8 slices of white bread, cut into circles with a cookie cutter
8 slices of smoked salmon
8 cooked large shrimps, peeled

Capers cream:
½ cup mayonnaise
¼ sour cream
2 tsp. capers, chopped
1 tbsp. chopped chives
2 tsp. chopped dill
2 tsp. lemon juice
1 tsp. lemon zest

Garnish:
2 tbsp. Danish caviar or salmon roe

To make the sandwiches, combine butter, horseradish and sour cream; spread onto bread. Arrange smoked salmon and shrimps on bread. Combine remaining ingredients, except caviar, and mix well. Spoon cream onto smoked salmon and shrimps; spoon on caviar.

The Danish open-face sandwiches, also known as smørrebrød, are one of most famous features of the Danish kitchen. These delicious sandwiches were not found anywhere else, not even in the neighboring countries of Norway and Sweden until recently. Now they are popping up all over the world. There are hundreds of variations and new ones are constantly being composed.
Small open-faced sandwiches are good as appetizers at a dinner party. They can also be served at a casual party together with drinks.

Norway Lobster with Parsley

4 appetizer servings

1 quart water
1 tbsp. lemon juice
1 tsp. salt
8 Norway lobsters
½ cup chopped parsley
½ cup rapeseed oil
salt and freshly ground pepper

Garnish:
1 lemon, cut into wedges
Dill sour cream (see page 37)

To make the Norway lobster, bring water, lemon juice and salt to a boil. Place lobsters in boiling water and bring water to a boil again. Cover and remove pot from heat. Let lobsters remain in water 2 minutes before draining. Can be made the day before.

To serve, place lobsters belly side up, on a cutting board and cut in halves lengthwise. Mix parsley, oil, salt and pepper and spread mixture on lobsters. Grill them 2-3 minutes under a hot grill. Serve with lemon wedges and dill sour cream or another dip.

Golden and Red Beet Salad

6 salad servings or a side dish

4 tbsp. hazelnuts, divided
2 tbsp. vegetable oil
2 tsp. hazelnut oil
1 tbsp. apple cider vinegar
salt and freshly ground pepper
2 peeled medium golden beets
1 peeled small turnip
1 peeled carrot
2 peeled red apples, halved and cored
2 peeled medium red beets, with leaves
2 tbsp. coarsely chopped parsley

Garnish:
eatable flowers

To make the dressing, crush 2 tbsp. hazelnuts; place in a small bowl. Whisk oils and vinegar in and season dressing to taste with salt and pepper. Set aside.

To make the salad, thinly slice golden beets, turnip, carrot and apples using a mandolin. Place them in a large bowl together with parsley. Slice red beets last and place in a small bowl.

To serve, place 2-3 red beet leaves on a platter. Spoon 3 tbsp. of dressing over red beet slices in the small bowl; pour remaining dressing over vegetables in medium bowl. Toss to coat each. Season with salt and pepper. Arrange red beets on top of the leaves; spoon over any dressing from bowl. Top red beets with remaining vegetables. Garnish with remaining hazelnuts.

Potato Salad with Hot Smoked Trout and Lemon Mayonnaise

4 lunch servings

Dressing:
3 oz. vegetable oil
2 oz. lemon juice
1 tbsp. apple cider vinegar
½ cup chopped parsley
½ cup ramsons* or chives, finely chopped
kosher salt and freshly ground pepper
1 stalk celery, diced
1 tbsp. capers

Salad:
1 lb. new baby potatoes, scrubbed but not peeled
1 small head of Bibb/butter lettuce salad
8 oz. smoked rainbow trout or hot smoked/cooked salmon**, skin and bones removed
Lemon mayonnaise:
1 egg yolk
1½ oz. lemon juice
zest of 1 lemon
kosher salt and freshly ground pepper
3½ oz. rapeseed/corn oil

To make the dressing, place oil, lemon juice, vinegar, ramsons/chives, salt and pepper in a bowl and whisk until combined. Stir in parsley, celery and capers.
To make the salad, cook potatoes in a large pot of salted boiling water until tender. Drain and allow to cool 5 minutes before slicing. Add potatoes to dressing while still warm. Stir to combine.
To make lemon mayonnaise, place egg yolk, lemon juice and zest, salt and pepper in food processor. Process until blended. With the machine running, slowly add the oil in a thin stream and process until emulsified.
To serve, divide salad among 4 plates, top with flaked smoked trout/salmon and drizzle with lemon mayonnaise.

* Ramsons (also known as wild garlic) have a garlicky, green flavor and can be found in the forests and fields growing wild in the early spring till the middle of June. They can also be found at the farmers market.

** If hot smoked trout or hot smoked salmon can't be found, cooked salmon is also good in this salad.

Chilled Leek Soup with Herbs

6 soup servings

2 tbsp. rapeseed oil
4 large thinly sliced leeks (white and pale green parts only)
1 large russet potato, peeled, cut into ½ inch cubes
4-5 cups vegetable broth
sea salt and freshly ground pepper

Garnish:
1 tbsp. very thinly sliced lemon peel (yellow part only)
1 tbsp. thinly sliced leek, (dark part only)
Fresh dill, coriander flowers, lemon thyme with flowers

To make the soup, heat oil in heavy, large pot over medium heat. Add leeks and cook until softened and wilted, stirring often, 5-6 minutes. Add potato; stir to coat. Add broth, increase heat to high, and bring to boil. Reduce heat to medium and simmer until vegetables are very tender, about 15 minutes.
Working in batches, purée soup in a blender until smooth. Season to taste with sea salt and pepper. Cover and chill.
To serve, divide soup among 4 bowls. Sprinkle with leeks, lemon, dill, coriander flowers, lemon thyme flowers or whatever you have in the garden or can find at the market.

Beet Sprouts and Nasturtium Salad with Shaved Hazelnuts

4 salad servings

Dressing:
½ cup rapeseed oil
2 tbsp. fresh lemon juice
kosher salt

Salad:
2 heads Bibb lettuce/butter lettuce
1 cup mixed flat-leaf parsley
1 cup nasturtium leaves
1 cup blood bull leaves (optional)
1 cup beet sprouts

Garnish:
5 blanched hazelnuts

To make the dressing, whisk oil and lemon juice in a bowl. Season with salt.
To make the salad, arrange lettuce, parsley, nasturtium leaves, blood bull leaves and beet sprouts on serving platter; spoon dressing over and sprinkle with shaved hazelnuts.

Whatever greens you find in your garden or at the market will be perfect in this salad. The idea is to use any salad types or eatable weeds you like. If you use dandelions from your garden, they should be new, small shoots and not the large old ones. Goutweed can also be used. Be sure to rinse them thoroughly and dry them carefully before using.

Red Currant Glazed Grilled Pork Chops and Salad with Red Currant Dressing

4 main course servings

6 oz. red currants
3 oz. sugar
Pork chops
4 6 oz. pork chops with bone, 1 inch thick
1 tbsp. oil

Salad with red currant dressing:
1 portion of mixed greens
1 tsp. honey
3 tbsp. apple cider vinegar
3 tbsp. rapeseed oil
2 oz. red currants

To make the red currant glace, place red currants and sugar in a sauce pan with 1 tbsp. water. Bring to boil and simmer 10 minutes. Strain, but do not press or force liquid through.
Prepare a fire in a charcoal grill or preheat gas grill to medium.
To grill the pork chops, brush them with oil, season with salt and grill 3-4 minutes. Turn them over and grill 3-4 minutes longer. Brush with red currant glace and grill them 1-2 minutes more. Be careful they don't burn. Transfer pork chops to a platter and brush again with the remaining red currant glaze.
To make the salad, place the mixed greens in a bowl. Whip honey, vinegar and oil together and pour over salad. Sprinkle with red currants.

Suggested accompaniment: pan roasted potatoes with rosemary.

Fish Cakes with Spinach Salad

4 main course servings

2 lb. cod fillets
3 eggs
4 tbsp. flour
½ cup milk
½ cup light cream
6 oz. shrimps
12 slices of bacon
1 tsp. fine salt
a dash of white pepper
butter with a few drops of rapeseed oil for frying
1 lemon cut in wedges

Salad:
1 lb. baby spinach
1 small salad onion cut in thin slices
2-3 tbsp. rapeseed oil

To make the fish cakes, cut fish into small pieces and chop with a sharp knife until fish is minced as coarsely or finely as you like. (The fish can be minced in a food processor, but it will be very fine). Add eggs, flour and stir in milk and cream a little at a time.
Add the whole shrimps to mixture. Fry bacon for both fish cakes and salad, crumble two slices and add to fish mixture. Save fat from bacon and the rest of the bacon for the salad. Season with fine salt and white pepper. Melt butter in a large skillet and add a few drops of rapeseed oil. Dip a spoon in fat before taking a scoop of mixture. Shape mixture into a flattened ball or cake in the palm of your hand. Place cakes in pan as you make them. Fry them over low heat 5 minutes, turn them and fry them 5 minutes on the other side.
To make the salad, rinse spinach and place in a large bowl. Heat bacon fat in skillet and add rapeseed oil to pan. Pour fat mixture over spinach, crumble remaining bacon and add both bacon and onions to the salad. Toss salad.
To serve, arrange fish cakes on 4 warmed plates with lemon and serve salad separately.

Suggested accompaniment: boiled new potatoes.

Garfish with Pea Purée

4 main course servings

Pea purée:
3 cups fresh, shelled peas (from 2 lb. peas in pod) or frozen peas, thawed, divided
kosher salt
1¾ cup fresh spinach leaves
4 tsp. vegetable oil
a large pinch of sugar
salt and freshly ground pepper
2 cups fresh pea tendrils* or pea sprouts, divided

Garfish:
4 6 oz. garfish fillets
1-2 tbsp. vegetable oil

To make the pea purée, cook peas in a large pot of boiling salted water for 1 minute. Using a slotted spoon, transfer to a large bowl of ice water. Boil spinach in same pot until wilted, 5-10 seconds. Transfer to bowl with peas in ice water. Reserve ½ cup of ice water. Drain pea mixture well and purée in a blender, adding reserved ice water by tablespoonfuls if mixture is too thick. Add oil and sugar; purée. Season to taste with salt and pepper.

To cook the garfish, season fish with salt. In a large nonstick sauté pan, heat oil over high heat, add garfish, skin down, and sauté until crisp and golden brown, 2 to 3 minutes; using a spatula, gently press on the fillet as it cooks so that the entire skin gets caramelized. Turn it over and cook for about 2 minutes.

To serve, warm purée over medium heat. Stir in reserved peas; cook until tender. Add half of pea tendrils; stir until wilted, about 1 minute. Divide pea mixture among plates and top with fish. Garnish with the rest of pea tendrils.

Suggested accompaniment: boiled new baby potatoes.

* Pea tendrils, the shoots and leaves that appear on the top of new pea plants, are tender little greens that taste like a cross between peas and spinach. They can be found in farmers' markets and special markets.

Crayfish with Farro Risotto

4 main course servings

6 quarts water
1½ quarts dark ale
6 sprigs of dill, plus extra for garnish
4 oz. salt
1 oz. sugar
2 tbsp. whole black peppercorns
1 lemon, cut into wedges
6 lbs. cleaned, live crayfish*

Risotto:
3-4 cups chicken stock
1 tbsp. butter
1 finely chopped onion
1 cup farro
¼ cup white wine
3 oz. salami, diced
salt and freshly ground pepper

Garnish:
dill, cress and pea shoots

To make the crayfish, place water, dark ale, dill, salt, sugar, peppercorns and lemon into a large pot and bring to a boil. Add crayfish and simmer 2-3 minutes. Drain and immerse in a bowl of ice water until cool; drain again.
To make the risotto, bring chicken stock to a simmer in medium saucepan. Cook salami in a large saucepan over medium heat until crisp. Transfer salami to paper towels to drain. Add onion to drippings in pan; cook until soft but not brown, stirring often, 4-5 minutes. Add farro to pan; stir 1-2 minutes. Add wine; stir until absorbed, about 2 minutes. Add ½ cup warm chicken stock to saucepan; stir until stock is absorbed, about 2 minutes. Repeat adding stock and stirring until farro is tender but still firm to bite and risotto is creamy, stirring almost constantly, about 20 minutes. Add salami and butter. Season to taste with salt and pepper.
To serve, divide risotto on 4 warmed plates. Garnish with cress and pea shoots. Place 1 or 2 crayfish on the plate. Place a large platter on the table with the remaining crayfish and let the guests serve themselves to more crayfish.

* To clean the crayfish, carefully pick each one up by grabbing it between the tail and body. If it's alive, it will raise its claws. Discard any that don't move. Scrub each with a kitchen brush under running water, especially the legs and under the tail. Grab the middle tail fin, twist it 180 degrees, and gently pull. This will remove the sandy intestinal tract. Throw that part away and place the cleaned crayfish in another bowl. Repeat to clean the remaining crayfish.

Roasted Turbot with Smoked New Baby Potatoes

4 main course servings

Smoked potatoes:
2 lbs. new baby potatoes, scrubbed clean, leave on skin
1 tbsp. salt
1 tbsp. corn oil
smoking sawdust
special equipment: an old pot with a lid

Turbot fillets:
6 tbsp. rapeseed/corn oil
4 7-8 oz. turbot fillets
salt and freshly ground white pepper

Sauce:
juice of 1 lemon
½ cup reduced fish stock
3 tbsp. heavy sour cream
5 oz. butter, diced
salt and freshly ground white pepper

To smoke the potatoes, cook potatoes in salted water 10-15 minutes. Drain and let potatoes steam dry. Add corn oil and make sure all potatoes are covered in oil.
Fill bottom of an old pot with smoking sawdust (1-2 cups depending on the size of pot). Place a large sheet of aluminum over sawdust. Fold edges up all the way around. Place potatoes in pot and place lid over. Turn on burner of stove. When pot begins to smoke, transfer pot outdoors and let stand with lid on 5 minutes.
To fry the turbot, heat 4 tbsp. of oil over medium-high heat. Season fish fillets with salt and white pepper and add them to the pan. Sauté on both sides until golden, 2-3 minutes. Transfer to a warmed large platter and tent with aluminum foil to keep warm.
To make the sauce, heat fish stock over medium-low heat and add sour cream and lemon juice. Whip constantly. Add butter a little at a time and season with salt and pepper.
To serve, arrange turbot on a platter with potatoes and serve the sauce separately.

Suggested accompaniment: a green salad or salad with herbs and creamy dressing (page 15).

Sautéed Plaice with Dill Potatoes

4 main course servings

Dill potatoes:
2 lb. new baby potatoes, scrubbed, with peel left on
1 bunch of dill
1 oz. butter
salt, Maldon or another good kosher salt

Plaice:
4 fresh whole plaice, with the skin removed
5-6 tbsp. dried bread crumbs, finely crumbled or flour
salt and freshly ground pepper
2 oz. butter
1 lemon cut in quarters

Garnish:
4 sprigs of dill

To make the potatoes, scrub them in cold water and place them in a pot with water just covering potatoes. Add stems of the dill and a handful of salt to the water. Cook potatoes 15-25 minutes depending on the type of potatoes. Drain.
To make the plaice, rinse in cold water, pat dry and with a sharp knife, make an incision all the way down the middle of the fish's back. This will prevent a super fresh fish from curling up while it is being fried.
Dredge fish in a mixture of breadcrumbs/flour, salt and pepper. Fry fish 3-4 minutes on each side in a large skillet two at a time in slightly browned butter over medium heat. Pour spoonfuls of melted butter from pan over thick end of fish while frying. This way the thin end and the thick end of the fish will be finished at the same time.
To serve, sprinkle potatoes with chopped dill and flakes of cold butter. Place plaice on warmed plates and some potatoes next to the fish. Place a lemon wedge on each plate and garnish with sprigs of dill.

Plaice with its characteristic red spots is the most plentiful fish in Northern Europe. Plaice is best in the summer and it is one of the most popular summer dishes in the North.

Chicken with Horseradish Sauce

6 main course servings

1 large chicken
1 onion, coarsely chopped
1 carrot, coarsely chopped
3 bay leaves
1½ tsp. black peppercorns
1 tsp. salt

Sauce:
1 tbsp. butter
1 tbsp. flour
16 oz. freshly shelled peas
1 bunch spring onions, coarsely chopped (save a little for the garnish)
1 cup heavy cream
2 tbsp. freshly grated horseradish
salt and freshly ground pepper

Garnish:
3-4 tbsp. chopped parsley
green part of spring onions, sliced
extra peas

To make the chicken, wash chicken in cold water, taking care to rinse out the body cavity well and put in a large pot. Fill pot with enough water to just cover chicken. Bring to a boil; skim off any foam. Add onion, carrot, bay leaves, peppercorns and salt. Bring back to a boil, decrease heat to a simmer. Simmer for 1 hr.
Transfer chicken to a plate and strain stock into a bowl. Measure 3 cups and set aside. Any leftover stock can be frozen and used another day.
To make the sauce, melt butter in a large skillet and stir flour in. Add 3 cups of stock a little at a time. Cook sauce 4 minutes and add peas and spring onions and let them cook 3 minutes before adding cream. Season to taste with salt, pepper and horseradish.
To serve, remove the meat from chicken. Add chicken to sauce and serve. Garnish with parsley, spring onions and peas.

Suggested accompaniment: boiled new baby potatoes and steamed carrots.

Ragout of Sweetbread, Wild Mushrooms and Smoked Ham

4 main course servings

20 oz. veal sweetbreads
3 tbsp. apple cider vinegar
2 tbsp. salt
1 tsp. freshly ground black pepper

Sauce:
1 tbsp. butter
2 tsp. apple cider vinegar
3 tbsp. white wine
3 cups veal stock or chicken stock
½ cup heavy cream
salt and freshly ground white pepper

Ragout:
1 tbsp. butter
3 oz. wild mushrooms, cleaned and cut into bite-size pieces
½ cup flour
3 tbsp. butter
2 tbsp. julienned smoked ham
1 tbsp. finely chopped fresh flat-leaf parsley
salt and freshly ground pepper

Garnish:
chervil sprigs or parsley

To prepare the sweetbreads, put them in 1 gallon of ice water to soak overnight; this will remove any blood left in them. The next day, bring 8 cups water to a boil in a large saucepan. Add vinegar, salt and pepper; lower heat to a low simmer, add the sweetbreads, and gently poach them for 4-5 minutes. Transfer sweetbreads to a bowl of ice water and let cool for 10 minutes. Drain and pat dry with a towel. Clean off any visible membrane or veins. Cut them in ½ inch thick pieces.
To make the sauce, melt butter in a large saucepan over medium heat. Add vinegar and wine, and bring to a boil. Add stock and cream and return to a boil. Season with salt and pepper. Set aside.
To make the ragout, melt butter in a sauté pan over high heat. Add mushrooms and sauté for 1-2 minutes. Dust sweetbreads with flour, season with salt and pepper. Melt butter in a skillet over high heat until hot. Add sweetbreads and sauté until crisp and golden brown, about 1-2 minutes per side. Transfer them to the sauce and add mushrooms, smoked ham and parsley. Bring to a boil, lower heat and simmer 1 minute. Season with salt and pepper.
To serve, spoon mashed potatoes first (if using) and spoon ragout over into 4 warmed shallow bowls. Top with chervil sprigs or parsley.

Suggested accompaniment: mashed potatoes.

Plum Marinated Grilled Chicken Breast with Cucumber Salad

4 main course servings

6 plums, pitted
2 oz. brown sugar
1 oz. honey
1 tbsp. apple cider vinegar
4 6 oz. boneless, skinless chicken breasts

Cucumber Salad:
1 large cucumber
1 cup apple cider vinegar
½ cup water
2-3 tbsp. sugar
salt and freshly ground pepper

To make marinade, place plums, brown sugar and honey in a skillet and melt sugar over medium heat. Add vinegar and cook 20 minutes. Puree marinade; place half of marinade in a medium bowl. Place the other half in a small bowl, cover and refrigerate to the next day.
Add chicken breasts to the medium bowl and toss to coat. Cover and refrigerate overnight.
To grill the chicken, heat a charcoal grill or broiler on medium heat. Remove chicken from marinade and season with salt. Grill lightly on both sides until well marked but still moist inside. Alternatively, broil for 8 minutes.
To make cucumber salad, wash and dry a large cucumber thoroughly. If it is a spring cucumber the green rind may be left on, but late in the season, when the rind may be thicker and harder, it is best to peel the cucumber. Cut cucumber in very thin slices with a sharp knife. Mix vinegar and water and sweeten to taste. Season with salt and pepper. Add cucumber slices. Let stand for at least 1 hour before serving.
To serve, arrange chicken on a platter together with the plum jam and serve the cucumber salad separately.

Suggested accompaniment: boiled new baby potatoes sprinkled with finely chopped parsley.

Honey and Blackberry Sorbet

6 dessert servings

1¾ cup water
½ cup honey
1 vanilla bean
1 lb. blackberries
1 tbsp. fresh lemon juice

Garnish:
2 oz. blackberries
2 oz. raspberries
2 tbsp. sugar
mint leaves

To make the sorbet, place water and honey in a saucepan. Split vanilla bean lengthwise, scrape seeds into pan, and add bean pod to pan. Bring to a boil, remove from heat. Remove bean pod. Let cool.
Add blackberries to saucepan, and transfer mixture to a food processor or blender and purée. Strain into a bowl. There should be 2 cups of strained juice. Add lemon juice, mix together thoroughly, and pour into an ice cream machine. Freeze according to manufacturer's directions.
To serve, sprinkle berries with sugar and place them on 6 plates. Place a scoop of sorbet in the middle of the berries. Garnish with mint leaves.

Red Berry Dessert

6 dessert servings

2 lbs. mixed fresh strawberries, red currants, black currants
½ lb. raspberries
½ cup water
8 oz. sugar
4-5 tbsp. cornstarch
3 cups ice cold heavy cream

To make the berries, put mixed berries in a pot and simmer gently for 5-6 minutes. Add sugar and cook briefly before adding the raspberries. Bring to a boil and stir, remove pot from heat. Dissolve cornstarch in a little cold water and mix it into boiling hot mixture. Bring mixture to a boil and remove from heat. Pour into a serving bowl and sprinkle a little sugar over to keep skin from forming.
To serve, divide dessert into 6 bowls and pour a little cream onto each bowl or let the guests pour as much cream as they want.

The season for each different type of berries in Denmark is short and intense. It is seldom that all the berries that grow in Denmark are ripe at the same time. Therefore, this dish, which is one of the most popular summer desserts in Denmark, can differ from week to week.

← Strawberries with Elderberry Crème

4 dessert servings

4 cups fresh strawberries, hulled and cut lengthwise in halves, depending on size
4 tbsp. concentrated elderberry juice, divided
2 egg yolks
1-2 tbsp. sugar
1 cup heavy cream

Garnish:
4 sprigs of mint
Elderflower*

To make the strawberries, place strawberries in a bowl; pour 2 tbsp. elderberry juice over and let marinate 30 minutes.
To make the crème, whisk yolks, sugar and juice until lightly colored. In another bowl, whisk heavy cream until it is stiff and forms peaks. Fold cream into egg mixture.
To serve, divide strawberries into 4 portions and arrange them on 4 plates; spoon a large spoonful cream over and garnish with mint.

* Tiny cluster of pale yellow or white flowers with a sweet, floral taste. The petals are great with strawberries and green salads.

Strawberry Ice Cream Sandwich

8 dessert servings

a good store bought Strawberry ice cream

Hazelnut cookies:
1 cup hazelnuts
½ cup flour
1 cup confectioner's sugar
4 oz. butter
1 egg yolk

Preheat oven to 400° F.
To make the cookies, place nuts in a blender and coarsely crush them. Place flour, sugar and butter in a bowl and with fingertips work butter into the dry ingredients. Add nuts and egg yolk and still working with hands, mix dough quickly and lightly. Place dough on a lightly floured board and roll it out. Cut out 16 circles with a glass or a cookie form. Bake cookies 10 minutes. Let them cool before assembling the sandwiches.
To assemble the sandwiches, place a spoonful of ice cream on 8 cookies. Place remaining cookies on top of ice cream and press them together. Serve immediately.

Autumn

Beet and Fennel Soup with Shaved Fennel and Sour cream

4 soup servings

2 tbsp. rapeseed oil
1 cup chopped onion
1 fennel bulb, save ¼ for shavings and chop coarsely remaining fennel
1½ tsp. fennel seeds
2 large beets, peeled, cut into ½ inch cubes
4 cups chicken broth
1 cup sour cream
salt and freshly ground pepper

Garnish:
4 tbsp. additional sour cream
fennel fronds

To make the soup, heat oil in a large pot over medium heat. Add onion, ¾ of the fennel and fennel seeds. Sauté until vegetables soften, about 5 minutes. Add beets and stir to coat. Add chicken broth and bring to a boil. Cover; reduce heat to medium-low. Cook until beets are tender, 18 to 20 minutes. Puree soup in batches in blender. Return to same saucepan. Whisk in 1 cup sour cream and season with salt and pepper. Rewarm soup.
To serve, pour soup into 4 bowls. Drizzle with additional sour cream; garnish with shavings of fennel and fennel fronds.

Warm Salad with Pumpkin, Chanterelles and Blue Cheese

→

6 appetizer servings

1 2 lbs. kabocha pumpkin*, butternut squash, or one pumpkin weighing 2 lb.
1 large or two small leeks, white and pale green parts only, chopped coarsely
10 oz. chanterelles, cleaned and cut into smaller pieces if they are very large
2 tbsp. rapeseed oil
salt and freshly ground pepper

Dressing:
1 tbsp. acacia honey
1 tbsp. apple cider vinegar

Garnish:
blue cheese
finely chopped parsley

To make the salad, cut rind off kabocha with a sharp knife. Cut kabocha into two pieces and scrape out the seeds with a spoon. Cut flesh into sticks ¼ inch thick and 2 inches long.
Heat oil in a large skillet and cook kabocha over medium-low heat 5 minutes. Transfer kabocha to a plate, and cook leaks and chanterelles in same skillet. Transfer leaks and chanterelles to plate with kabocha. Sprinkle with salt and pepper.
To make the dressing, whisk honey and vinegar together. Pour dressing onto kabocha, leeks and chanterelles and stir to combine.
To serve, divide salad onto 4 plates and crumble blue cheese over. Sprinkle with parsley.

* Kabocha pumpkins are sweeter and denser than pumpkins.

Mushroom Soup with Jerusalem Artichoke Chips

4 soup servings

Soup:

8 oz. wild mushrooms, chanterelles, oyster mushrooms, cleaned and cut into bite-size pieces, save 1 oyster mushroom for garnish and cut in thin slices
1 finely chopped onion
1 tbsp. butter
1 cup white wine
1 cup water
1½ cup chicken broth
1½ cup heavy cream
1-2 sprigs of thyme
2 oz. butter
salt and freshly ground pepper
2 tbsp. lemon juice

Garnish:

5-6 Jerusalem artichokes*, scrubbed, cut in very thin slices
oil for frying
4 sprigs of thyme

To make the soup, melt butter over high heat. Add onion and sauté 1-2 minutes. Add mushrooms and sauté 1-2 minutes. Add wine, water and broth; lower heat to a simmer and cook 5 minutes. Transfer mushrooms to a plate and reduce liquid by half. Add cream and thyme and reduce by half, 5-7 minutes. Reduce heat to low and gradually add butter, stirring slowly (do not whisk) until it is all incorporated. Season soup with salt, pepper and lemon.

Add cooked mushrooms and raw oyster mushroom slices and heat soup 2-3 minutes.

To make the Jerusalem artichoke chips, heat oil and fry Jerusalem artichoke slices crisp.

To serve the soup, pour soup into 4 bowls and garnish with Jerusalem artichoke chips. Place a sprig of thyme in each bowl.

*Jerusalem artichokes are also known as sunchokes.

Liver Mousse with Apple and Snaps*

Serves 16 as an appetizer

300 g chicken livers, trimmed of extra fat and sinew
3 oz. butter
salt and freshly ground pepper
1 finely chopped onion
1 apple, peeled, cored and diced
3 tbsp. snaps/aquavit*
white bread or Danish rye bread (recipe page 33)

Garnish:
1 apple, cored and cut into slices

To make the mousse, melt 1/3 of the butter and sauté liver 2-3 minutes. Season with salt and pepper. Remove liver from the pan and sauté onion and apple, 2-3 minutes. Return liver to pan, pour snaps over and bring to a boil. Remove pan and wait until lever mixture is cold. When mixture is cold, blend with the rest of the butter. Season with salt and pepper. Pour mousse into a bowl, cover with plastic film and set in refrigerator.
To serve, spread on toasted white or rye bread. (Recipe page 33). Garnish with slices of raw apple.

* Snaps, also known as aquavit, is a traditional flavored sprit and is a specialty of Denmark.

Mussels Cooked in Beer

4 appetizer servings

4 lb. mussels, scrubbed and debearded
1½ tbsp. rapeseed oil
2 finely chopped shallots
1 bottle of beer
1 cup heavy cream
salt and freshly ground pepper

Garnish:
Fresh mint

To make the mussels, heat a large heavy pot over high heat until very hot. Add oil and fry shallots; add mussels and beer. Cover and cook, stirring frequently, until mussels fully open (discard any that do not open). Using a slotted spoon, transfer mussels to 4 warmed bowls.
Add cream to pot, reduce soup by half. Season with salt and pepper and spoon over mussels.
To serve, garnish mussels with mint and serve immediately.

Savoy Cabbage with Blue Cheese Dressing, Walnuts and Blueberries

4 salad servings

1 small Savoy cabbage, shredded
3 oz. blue cheese
½ cup hazelnut oil
2 tbsp. white wine vinegar
1 oz. walnuts
3 oz. blueberries

To make the savoy salad, whisk a dressing of blue cheese, oil and vinegar and season with salt and pepper. Pour dressing over Savoy cabbage and toss.
To serve, sprinkle with walnuts and blueberries.

Venison Tartare with Sautéed Porcini and Porcini Mayonnaise

4 appetizer or lunch servings

500 g venison, bison or beef fillet
2 tbsp. butter
3 oz. fresh porcini mushrooms or another wild mushroom, cleaned and cut into bite-size pieces
1 oz. dried porcini mushrooms, divided
4 tbsp. homemade mayonnaise (see page 13) or a good mayonnaise
1-2 tbsp. Maldon salt
½ tbsp. freshly ground pepper
1-2 oz. fresh cranberries (optional)

Garnish:
fresh herbs such as cress, sorrel

To make the tartare, place meat in freezer 30 minutes before using. It makes it easier to work with. Scrape meat with a very sharp knife, along the length of the muscle tissue, so you get fine, long segments of meat. Ensure there is no sinew in the finished tartare. Place in a bowl and set aside.
To make the porcini mushrooms, melt butter in a skillet over medium-high heat. Add mushrooms and sauté 1-2 minutes. Season lightly with salt and pepper and set aside.
To make porcini mayonnaise, grind dried porcini to a very fine powder in a blender. Add half of ground porcini powder to mayonnaise and stir until porcini is absorbed.
To serve tartare, place meat on 4 plates. Sprinkle with salt and pepper. Arrange sautéed porcini on top and place 4-5 tsp. mayonnaise around and over tartare and porcini. Scatter fresh cranberries over and sprinkle with remaining porcini powder.

Suggested accompaniment: toasted rye bread (page 33).

Duck Breast with Apple Walnut Salad

4 main course servings

4 (8-9 oz.) duck breasts

Dressing:
½ cup walnut oil/corn oil
2 tbsp. apple cider vinegar
salt and freshly ground pepper

Salad:
1 cup rye bread (see page 33) cut in small cubes or coarse breadcrumbs
½ cup walnuts
2 crisp apples, halved and cored, thinly sliced
1 head Bibb lettuce/Butter lettuce
4 scallions, thinly sliced
½ cup fresh flat-leaf parsley leaves

To make the duck breasts, trim of any extra skin and score fat in a cross-hatch pattern.
Heat a large sauté skillet over high heat until hot, add duck, skin side down, and cook for 8-10 minutes (depending on thickness of breast). Turn duck over, and cook 5-8 minutes. Remove duck from heat and let rest 3 minutes.
To make the dressing, whisk oil and vinegar together in a small bowl. Season with salt and pepper. Set aside. Preheat oven to 350°F.
To make the croutons, spread rye bread/breadcrumbs on a small rimmed baking sheet; stirring occasionally, until crisp, 6-8 minutes. Let cool and set aside.
To make the walnuts, spread them on a small rimmed baking sheet; toast, stirring occasionally, until golden brown, 5-6 minutes. Let cool; coarsely chop.
To serve, toss breadcrumbs, walnuts, apples, scallions, parsley and lettuce in a large bowl. Drizzle with dressing, toss again. Divide the salad among 4 plates. Slice the duck breast and arrange on plate next to salad.

Salted Cod with Warm Vegetable Sauce

8 appetizers

3 lb. cod fillet, with the skin left on

Marinade:
2 quarts water
2 cups sugar
1½ cup kosher salt
1 tbsp. coarsely cracked pepper
1 tbsp. coarsely cracked coriander
1 tbsp. juniper berries, cracked
5-6 sprigs of dill
3 bay leaves

Sauce:
1 coarsely chopped carrot
¼ coarsely chopped celery root
1 coarsely chopped leek
1 coarsely chopped onion
2 tbsp. rapeseed oil
½ cup white wine
2 cups fish broth
2 cups heavy cream
1 tbsp. finely chopped thyme
1 pinch saffron

Garnish:
cress or dill

To make the cod, carefully remove all the bones. Place cod skin side up in a deep dish.
Combine ingredients to marinade and bring to a boil. Pour over cod, cover and refrigerate for at least 24 hours.
Next day, cut the cod in very thin slices diagonally across the grain.
To make the sauce, place carrot, celery root, leek and onion in a food processor and process to a fine mixture. Warm oil in a large saucepan over medium heat; add vegetable mixture and sauté until soft. Add wine and cook until almost absorbed. Add fish broth, heavy cream, thyme and saffron; cook until sauce is reduced by half.
To serve, place 1 or 2 spoonfuls of the warm sauce on a plate and place 2-3 slices of cod in the middle of the plate. Warm sauce – cold fish. Garnish with cress or dill.

Sole with Mussels and Saffron Sauce

4 main course servings

Stuffing:
10 oz. salmon, skin removed
1 egg
1 finely chopped carrot
¼ finely chopped celery root
1 finely chopped leek
2 tbsp. butter
salt and freshly ground pepper

Mussels:
20-25 mussels, scrubbed and debearded
½ bottle dry white wine

Sole fillets:
12 small sole fillets, skins removed

Saffron sauce:
½ quart mussel stock
½ quart heavy cream
1 pinch saffron
salt and freshly ground pepper
juice of a freshly squeezed lemon

Garnish:
4 sprigs of thyme, parsley or chives

To make the stuffing, place salmon and egg in a food processor and blend. Melt butter in a skillet and sauté vegetables 4-5 minutes. Add vegetables to salmon mixture. Season with salt and pepper. Set aside.
To make the mussels, combine mussels and wine in a large, heavy nonreactive pot over high heat. Cover and cook, shaking pot occasionally, until mussels open, 4-5 minutes. Discard any mussels that do not open. Drain; reserving mussel stock. Shell all of the mussels, leaving 12 mussels in their shells. Strain reserved mussel stock through a fine-mesh sieve.
To make the fish, spread salmon stuffing on each fillet and fold left side over the middle and then fold right side over forming a small package. Turn packages over and place them in a shallow skillet in a single layer and pour enough mussel stock so packages are covered. Cover skillet and simmer packages over medium heat for 5-6 minutes, until they are just cooked.
With a slotted spoon, transfer packages to a warm serving dish. Cover and keep warm while making the sauce.
To make the sauce, add mussel stock and heavy cream to pot. Cook over medium-high heat until reduced to 3 cups, stirring occasionally. Add saffron and season with salt, pepper and lemon juice to taste.
To serve, arrange two or three fillets on each plate; pour sauce over and place three mussels in half shells on each plate. Scatter any leftover mussels on the plate. Garnish with thyme.

Suggested accompaniment: boiled fingerling potatoes.

Roasted Pheasant Breast with Savoy Cabbage and Salsify

4 main course servings

2 oz. bacon, finely chopped
8 spears of salsify, scrubbed and trimmed
1½ cup heavy cream
½ cup vegetable bouillon
2 oz. butter
¼ Savoy cabbage or white cabbage, shredded
salt and freshly ground pepper

Pheasant:
4 pheasant breasts, about 2 lb.
2 tbsp. butter
2 tbsp. rapeseed oil
1 tsp. thyme, finely chopped
salt and freshly ground pepper

Garnish:
4 sprigs of thyme

To make salsify, cook bacon in a skillet over medium-low heat until the fat is reduced, then add the salsify, cream and bouillon. Cover and cook 5-10 minutes depending on how thick the salsify are. Transfer salsify to a plate and hold them warm. Strain cream, return to skillet and add the butter and stir until butter is incorporated with the cream.
To make the cabbage, cook cabbage in a pot of salted water 5 minutes. Strain cabbage and sprinkle with salt and pepper.
To make the pheasant, melt butter and add oil over medium-high heat. Add breast, skin side up and sauté until golden, about 2 minutes. Turn them so they are skin side down and sauté 5 minutes. Pour enough stock into skillet to come halfway up the sides of the pheasant breasts, add thyme and bring to a simmer. When breasts are fully cooked but still moist, transfer to a plate and hold them warm. Sprinkle with salt and pepper.
To serve, slice the pheasant on the diagonal and fan the slices over a mound of cabbage on 4 warm plates. Warm sauce carefully and spoon around the plate. Place 2 salsify next to the breasts. Garnish with a sprig of thyme.

Suggested accompaniment: fingerling potatoes.

Roast Chicken with Parsnips, Golden Beets and Jerusalem Artichokes

4 main course servings

1 4 lb. chicken
3 fresh sprigs of thyme plus 1 tbsp. chopped fresh thyme, divided
2½ tsp. coarse kosher salt
1 tbsp. rapeseed oil
3 golden beets, peeled, cut into wedges
4 tsp. vegetable oil
1 lb. parsnips, peeled, quartered lengthwise, cut crosswise into 1½ inch pieces
5-6 oz. Jerusalem artichokes, scrubbed, halved lengthwise, cut crosswise into 1 inch pieces
1 cup lager or pale ale
salt and freshly ground pepper

To make the chicken, slide 1 thyme sprig under the skin of each chicken breast. Sprinkle with ½ tsp. coarse salt inside cavity of the chicken and place 1 thyme sprig in the cavity. Sprinkle outside of chicken all over with remaining salt. Place chicken on a plate. Let stand uncovered at room temperature 2 hours or cover and chill overnight.
Preheat oven to 450° F.
To make the vegetables, place beets, parsnips and Jerusalem artichokes in a bowl. Add 4 tsp. of oil and chopped herbs, sprinkle with salt and pepper. Toss vegetables and place them in a large oven proof casserole and place chicken in the middle of vegetables. Roast chicken and vegetables 20 minutes. Reduce heat to 375° F and roast 50-60 minutes. Turn the vegetables occasionally.
To serve, transfer chicken to a platter and arrange vegetables around the chicken. Place casserole on stove top and add beer. Bring to a boil, scraping the browned bits, 3-4 minutes. Season with salt and pepper. Transfer juices to small pitcher. Serve chicken and vegetables, passing the pan juices alongside.

Pork Cheeks with Jerusalem Artichoke Purée and Chips

4 main course servings

2 tbsp. duck fat
12 pork cheeks, trimmed for fat and sinew
½ head of celery root, peeled and cut into smaller pieces
3-4 carrots, coarsely chopped
1 onion, coarsely chopped
1 bottle of dark beer

Jerusalem artichoke purée and chips:
8 Jerusalem artichokes*, scrubbed, 7 cut into 1 inch cubes, one artichoke sliced thinly
1 cup whole milk
1 onion, coarsely chopped
1 cup heavy cream
salt and freshly ground pepper

Garnish:
fried parsley (optional)
oil for frying chips and parsley
8-12 sprigs of parsley

To make the pork cheeks, melt duck fat in a large heavy pot over medium-high heat. Brown meat, turning until browned on all sides 8-10 minutes. Add celery root, carrots, onions and beer to pot. Bring to boil over high heat, reduce heat to medium, cover. Braise pork cheeks 1½-2 hours until a knife slides easily through meat.
To make the artichoke purée, place artichoke cubes and onion in a heavy, large pot. Add milk and enough water to cover. Sprinkle with salt. Bring to boil, reduce heat to medium and simmer with lid slightly ajar until tender, 15-20 minutes. Drain; return to pot. Stir over medium heat to dry. Using potato masher, mash artichokes until coarsely purée. Stir heavy cream in and season with salt and pepper. The purée should not be firm, add milk or water if the purée is too stiff.
To make the artichoke chips, heat oil to 360°F and deep fry artichokes chips until golden brown and crispy, 2-3 minutes. Drain on paper towels and season with salt.
To make the fried parsley, use the same oil, deep fry parsley 1-2 minutes. Drain on paper towels.
To serve, divide pork cheeks and artichoke purée on 4 warmed plates. Garnish with chips and fried parsley.

* Jerusalem artichokes (also called sun chokes) are the tubers of a variety of sunflower.

Pork Shanks with Red Beets and Blueberries

4 main course servings

2 (3 lbs. each) pork shanks*
1 cup diced carrots
1 cup diced leeks
1 cup diced onion
2 tsp. minced garlic
2-3 sprigs of thyme
2-3 sage leaves
2 bay leaves
10 black peppercorns
2 cups vegetable broth
1 dark beer

Beets:
4 red beets
3-4 oz. coarse salt
1 tbsp. rapeseed oil
½ tbsp. apple cider vinegar
3 oz. blueberries
chopped fresh thyme

Sauce:
2 tbsp. butter
2 tbsp. apple cider vinegar
salt and freshly ground pepper

Preheat oven to 425°F.
To make the pork shanks, score fat in a cross-hatch pattern in rind without cutting into the meat itself. Brown shanks in the warm oven 10-15 minutes. until shanks begin to caramelize. Place pork in a large heavy ovenproof pot with a tight fitting lid; arrange carrots, leeks, onion, garlic, thyme, sage, peppercorns and bay leaves around the pork. Add broth and beer. Bring to a boil over high heat, cover and transfer to the oven.
Reduce the heat to 300°F and braise 1½-2 hours.
To make the red beets, wash 4 beets and place them in a roasting pan no larger than just enough to hold them. Cover beets with salt. Set beets in oven next to shanks and bake 1½ hours. Transfer beets to a plate and let them cool off. When they are cool, remove skins and slice them in thin slices. Whisk rapeseed oil and vinegar together with thyme, salt and pepper in a bowl. Add blueberries and beets to bowl and toss so that blueberries and beets are covered.
To make the sauce, transfer shanks to a plate. Strain braising liquid into a pot and cook over high heat until reduced by half. Add apple cider vinegar and whisk butter in. Season to taste with salt and pepper.
To serve, place shanks on a platter and arrange beets and blueberries around shanks. Garnish with thyme sprigs. Pass the sauce separately.

Suggested accompaniment: mashed potatoes.

* Depending on the size of the shanks, two may not be enough for 4 people. If the dinner guests are 4 young men, count on a shank for each person.

Venison Ragout with Walnuts and Celery Fries

8 main course servings

3 lbs. venison rump roast (beef can be substituted)
2 tbsp. flour
4 tbsp. butter
3 chopped onions
1 chopped carrot
1 chopped celery stalk
1 thyme sprig
2 bay leaves
2 cups red wine
4 cups venison stock (see page 107) veal or chicken stock
salt and freshly ground pepper

Garnish:
1 tbsp. butter
1 celery stalk sliced into thin strips
2 oz. walnuts

Celery fries:
1 celery head
3 oz. duck fat
vegetable oil for deep frying

To make the ragout, cut meat into cubes 1 x 1 inch and 1¼ inches thick. Dust meat lightly with flour. Melt butter in a large skillet and brown meat. Transfer meat to a plate and sauté vegetables. Add red wine, stock, thyme sprig and bay leaves to pot. Season with salt and pepper. Place meat in sauce and let simmer with lid on 1-1½ hour. Transfer meat to a plate. Remove lid and reduce the sauce by half.
To make the garnish, melt butter and sauté celery strips and walnuts 1-2 minutes. Season with salt and pepper.
To make the fries, peel and cut celery into sticks ¼ inch thick and 3 inches long; keep them in cold water until ready to fry.
To fry, drain celery sticks and pat them dry with a paper towel. Melt duck fat in a large skillet and fry celery sticks over low heat until soft but not colored or crisp, about 5 minutes. Using a slotted metal spoon, transfer fries to paper towels to drain. Repeat with remaining celery sticks. Set aside.
To finish cooking fries, heat oil to 360°F and deep fry celery sticks again until golden brown and crispy, 2-3 minutes. Drain on paper towels and season with salt.
To serve, divide celery fries among 8 warmed plates. Spoon ragout onto plates and garnish with celery and walnuts.

The secret of good celery fries is frying them twice. First at a low temperature to blanch and cook the celery, then a higher temperature to crisp and color them. They should be soft in the center and crisp outside.

Cider Brined Pork Roast with Roasted Apples and Baked Onions

8 main course servings

Filling:
2 tbsp. butter
1 cup minced onion
2 tsp. dried thyme
½ tsp. freshly ground pepper
1 lb. ground pork

Pork:
1 trimmed 2½-3 lb. pork loin
1 tsp. kosher salt
½ tsp. freshly ground pepper
1 bunch parsley, stemmed and chopped coarsely
4 oz. sliced Danish dry cured ham or prosciutto
5 bay leaves
8 small apples, halved and cored
3 tbsp. butter, divided
2 tbsp. rapeseed oil
1 cup apple cider
½ cup chicken stock

Roasted onions:
4 large white onions, unpeeled
4 large red onions, unpeeled
8 small shallots, unpeeled
kosher salt

To make the filling, melt butter in a large skillet over medium heat. Add onion; cook, stirring often, until soft and lightly golden, about 8 minutes. Stir in thyme; cook for 1 minute. Stir in 2 tsp. salt and ½ tsp. pepper. Transfer mixture to a bowl and let cool completely. Add ground pork and stir to combine.

To make the roast, put pork on a work surface with short end facing you. Holding a long, thin sharp knife parallel to work surface and beginning along one long side, cut ½ inch above underside of roast. Continue slicing inward, pulling back the meat with your free hand and unrolling the roast like a carpet, until the entire loin is flat. Using a meat mallet, pound to an even thickness.

Season with 1 tsp. salt and ½ tsp. pepper. Scatter parsley over meat. Spread filling on top of parsley leaving a 1 inch border. Roll pork into a tight cylinder. Wrap one layer of dry cured ham around the roast. Tie roast securely with kitchen twine in 1½ inch intervals.* Tuck bay leaves under twine.

Preheat oven to 400°F.

To cook roast, place apples in a pan. Melt 1 tbsp. butter with oil in a large skillet. Brown pork on all sides and place in pan next to apples. Add cider and ½ cup stock to skillet and bring to a boil, scraping the browned bits. Pour mixture into roasting pan. Roast pork until an instant-read thermometer inserted into the center of loin reads 145°F, 45-60 minutes.

To make the onions, cut white onions, red onions and shallots almost in half, leaving root ends intact. Pry each open slightly to expose cut side. Place white and red onions root side down (if they won't stand up, slice the bottom so it is flat) on a baking sheet next to the pork loin after the pork has been in the oven 1 hour. Roast onions 40 minutes until just beginning to soften and brown. Remove the pork. It will be cooked medium but still slightly pink, about 1 hour. Let roast rest at least 20 minutes. Add shallots to baking sheet and roast until onions and shallots are soft, 20-30 minutes. Season with salt.

To serve, transfer roast and apples to a platter. Pour juices into a pan and add chicken stock and cook 5 minutes until slightly thickened. Whisk in remaining 2 tbsp. butter and season to taste with salt and pepper. Strain sauce; slice pork. Serve sauce, apples and onions alongside sliced pork.

* Loop the free end of a ball of string round the end of the meat and tie a knot. Without cutting the string, make successive loops at 1½ inch intervals along the meat; tighten each loop by pulling the string as you go. Secure the parcel by bringing the string under the entire length of the meat and knotting the free end.

Denmark has dry cured ham with the same quality as the Italian prosciutto and the Spanish Serrano ham. If you can't find Danish dry cured ham, either one of these can be used.

Pancakes with Buttermilk Mousse and Blackberries

4-6 dessert servings

Buttermilk mousse:
2 tbsp. powdered gelatin
2 tbsp. water
2½ cups buttermilk
3 tbsp. sugar
1 tsp. vanilla extract
1 cup heavy cream

Pancakes:
Approx. 12 pancakes
1 cup flour
1 tsp. sugar
¼ tsp. salt
3 eggs
2 cups milk
grated peel of 1 lemon
3 tbsp. beer or water
butter

Elderberry syrup:
1 cup elderberry juice

Garnish:
Blackberries, blueberries or another berry

To make buttermilk mousse, pour 4 tbsp. water into a small saucepan. Sprinkle in powdered gelatin. Heat mixture over low heat, stirring continuously until gelatin has dissolved. Let cool. Stir buttermilk with sugar and vanilla extract. Pour gelatin into buttermilk mixture. Place mousse in refrigerator until almost stiff, 15-20 minutes. Beat cream until stiff peaks form and take mousse out of the refrigerator. Fold carefully whipped cream into mousse and pour mousse into a bowl. Set mousse in refrigerator until dessert should be assembled.
To make pancakes, combine flour, sugar, salt and grated lemon peel. Beat eggs and mix them with flour and a little milk. Whisk in remaining milk together with beer and beat until smooth.
Melt butter and brush a little on the bottom of a small skillet. Pour enough batter to thinly cover the bottom and cook the pancakes until underside is brown; turn and brown the other side. Repeat until all the batter is used. Place pancakes on a plate.
To make elderberry syrup, cook juice in a small saucepan 15 minutes or until it is thick. Not too thick, as it will thicken when it is cooled.
To serve, place 1 or 2 large spoonfuls of mousse in the middle of a pancake and fold one side over and then the second side over the mousse so that it resembles a tube with mousse inside. Drizzle elderberry syrup over pancakes and garnish with blackberries, blueberries or another berry of your choice.

Roasted Pears with Lavender Sugar, Blackberries and Ice cream

6 dessert servings

4 tbsp. sugar
1 tbsp. dried lavender blossoms
6 ripe, unpeeled pears, quartered, cored
2 tbsp. fresh lemon juice
1 lb. fresh blackberries
2 cups vanilla ice cream

Garnish:
2-3 sprigs of fresh lavender (optional)

To make the pears, grind sugar and lavender blossoms in a food processor until lavender is finely chopped.
Preheat broiler. Generously butter large rimmed baking sheet. Toss pears, lemon juice and 1 tbsp. lavender sugar in a large bowl. Place pears skin side down on baking sheet. Broil until pears begin to caramelize, about 5-6 minutes. Arrange berries around pears; sprinkle with 1 tbsp. lavender sugar. Broil until berries begin to release juice, about 5 minutes.
To serve, divide pears, berries, and juice among 6 bowls. Top with a dollop of ice cream, sprinkle with fresh lavender and serve.

Licorice Mousse

6 dessert servings

1 cup dark beer (e.g. IPA dark)
2 cups heavy cream
4 tbsp. sugar
1 tbsp. licorice powder
2 tbsp. powdered gelatin

Garnish:
whipped cream
powdered sugar

To make the mousse, cook beer with sugar and cream. Whip licorice in. Remove from the heat.
Place 4 tbsp. of water in a small saucepan. Sprinkle in powdered gelatin. Heat mixture over low heat, stirring continuously until gelatin has dissolved. Let it cool; then pour into licorice mixture. Pour licorice into a serving bowl or 6 small bowls. Refrigerate mousse for at least 4 hours or as long as 24 hours before serving.
To serve, garnish with whipped cream and sprinkle powdered sugar over. A very small amount of licorice powder can be sprinkled over the dessert, but be very careful. Don't use too much powder, it can be very strong.

Apple Cake with Hazelnuts and Lavender

8 dessert servings

2 eggs
1 cup sugar
3 oz. hazelnuts, crushed slightly
2 apples, peeled, cored and cut into wedges
4 tbsp. flour
2 tsp. baking powder
1 cup heavy cream

Garnish:
sprigs of lavender
extra hazelnuts

Preheat oven to 350°F.
To make the cake, whisk eggs with sugar until smooth. Fold hazelnuts, apples, flour and baking powder into the cake. Pour cake batter into a buttered baking pan. Bake cake 35 minutes.
To serve, let cake cool slightly. Whip cream until soft peaks form. Top cake with cream and sprinkle with shaved hazelnuts. Garnish with lavender.

Winter

Spice-Cured Veal with Pear salad

Serves 8 as appetizers

3 tbsp. kosher salt
3 tbsp. sugar
2 tsp. ground all spice
2 tsp. ground cloves
3 veal cutlets, approx. 1½ lb.
½ cup Danish snaps/aquavit*

Pear and Jerusalem artichoke salad:
10 oz. Jerusalem artichokes**
2 pears, halved and cored
2 tbsp. grated fresh horseradish
2 oz. raisins
1 lemon, juice and zest
½ tbsp. sugar
1 tsp. fine salt
1 tbsp. rapeseed oil

To make the veal, mix salt, sugar, and spices. Coat veal slices in half of mixture. Pour snaps/aquavit over and place meat in a plastic bag. Let veal marinate in refrigerator 2 hours. Discard snaps/aquavit and coat veal slices in rest of salt/sugar/spices mixture. Place meat in bag again and let marinate 2 more hours.
To make the salad, scrub Jerusalem artichokes and slice them together with pears in thin slices. Whisk a dressing of horseradish, lemon juice and zest, raisins, sugar, salt and oil. Pour dressing over artichokes and pears.
To serve, slice veal in thin slices and place on a plate. Arrange Jerusalem artichokes and pear salad on top of the meat.

Suggested accompaniment: bread, toasted Danish rye bread (see page 33).

* Snaps, also known as aquavit, is a traditional flavored sprit and is a specialty of Denmark.

** Jerusalem artichokes are also known as sunchokes.

Salt Cured Salmon with Apple and Horseradish Salad

10 appetizer servings

1 2 lb. salmon filet with skin
3 tbsp. fine salt
1 tbsp. sugar

Salad:
4 tbsp. rapeseed oil
4 tbsp. apple juice
1 finely chopped shallot
2 tbsp. freshly grated horseradish
1 small apple, quartered, cored and diced

Garnish:
a handful of fresh herbs, dill and cress

To make the fish, remove all bones and place salmon in deep dish skin side down. Sprinkle with salt and sugar. Cover and refrigerate till the next day.
To make the dressing, whisk together a marinade of oil, apple juice, shallot, and horseradish in a small bowl. Add diced apple to marinade and toss.
To serve, cut salmon in very thin slices diagonally across the grain and place them on a serving plate. Arrange salad on top. Garnish with herbs.

This salmon can be served in all seasons. In the summer, it would be nice garnished with cucumbers and radishes instead of apple and horseradish salad.

The technique of curing fatty fish evolved from a pre refrigeration era need to preserve seafood in a safe, flavorful way. The salt in the cure (a mix of salt and sugar in this recipe and herbs, spices and citrus zest in other recipes) draws out moisture, transforming the texture and color of the fish. After a few hours or days in the refrigerator, the fish loses 15% of its weight. The condensed flesh takes on a reddish hue and a glossy sheen.

Salad with Raw Marinated Jerusalem Artichokes and Dried Cranberries

8 salad servings

1 lb. Jerusalem Artichokes*
3 tbsp. apple cider vinegar
2 tbsp. rapeseed oil
4 finely chopped small shallots
1 small head Bibb salad
2 oz. dried cranberries
salt and freshly ground pepper

Garnish:
parsley leaves

To make the salad, scrub Jerusalem Artichokes and slice them on a mandolin. Place slices in a bowl. Whisk a dressing of vinegar, oil and ½ tsp. salt and pour over the Jerusalem Artichokes. Let stand 30 minutes.
To serve, place salad leaves and parsley on 4 plates and arrange Jerusalem Artichokes on top of salad. Sprinkle chopped shallots and cranberries over.

*Jerusalem artichokes are also known as sunchokes.

Salt Cured Duck Breast and Jerusalem Artichokes Salad

→

8 servings as an appetizer

2 1-lb. boneless duck breasts with skin

Salt mixture:
2 cups kosher salt
1½ cup packed dark brown sugar
10 cracked juniper berries
15 cracked cloves
4-5 bay leaves
1 tsp. coarsely cracked black peppercorns

To make the duck, cut the skin with parallel slits without cutting into meat. Mix remaining ingredients in a medium bowl. Arrange 2 sheets of plastic wrap side by side on a work surface. Spread 1 scant cup salt mixture (do not pack) in center of each sheet, spreading mixture to match the size of the duck breasts. Top each with 1 duck breast, skin side down. Spread remaining salt mixture over meat, dividing equally. Bring plastic wrap up and over each duck breast, wrapping tightly. Place on a small rimmed plate, skin side down and refrigerate for 7 days to cure.
To serve, unwrap duck breasts. Scrape off salt mixture, (do not rinse). Using a long, sharp knife, thinly slice meat. Arrange on 4 plates or a large platter. Serve with fresh figs, chutney or a salad.

Salt

Celery Root and Apple Salad with Hazelnut Dressing

4-6 salad servings

Dressing:
1 tbsp. Dijon mustard
2 tbsp. apple cider vinegar
1 tbsp. freshly squeezed lemon juice
½ tsp. salt
¼ cup hazelnut oil plus additional for drizzling
2 tbsp. grape oil

Salad:
1 medium celery root, peeled, cut into matchstick-size strips
1 medium fennel bulb, halved lengthwise, thinly sliced
1 unpeeled apple, cut into strips
2 tbsp. finely chopped hazelnuts

To make the dressing, whisk the first 4 ingredients in a small bowl. Whisk in hazelnut oil and grape oil.
To make the salad, combine celery root, fennel and apple in a large bowl. Toss with dressing.
To serve, divide among 4-6 plates and sprinkle with chopped hazelnuts. Drizzle with additional hazelnut oil.

Chickpea Soup with Broccoli

6 soup servings

1½ cup dried chickpeas or 3 15-oz. cans chickpeas, rinsed
3 tbsp. rapeseed oil
2 large coarsely chopped onions
4 chopped garlic cloves
1 sprig of thyme
½ cup dry white wine
4 cups vegetable broth
kosher salt and freshly ground pepper
1 bunch broccoli, stems reserved for another use, cut into small florets

Garnish:
4 tbsp. sour cream
4 sprigs of thyme

To make the soup if using dried chickpeas, place in medium bowl and add cold water to cover by 2 inches. Let soak overnight in refrigerator. Drain chickpeas.
To cook the soup, heat oil in a large heavy pot over medium heat. Add onions, garlic and thyme sprig; cook, stirring occasionally, until onions are soft. Add chickpeas and wine. Bring to a rapid simmer; cook until wine is reduced by half, about 2 minutes. Add broth and bring to a boil. Reduce heat, cover, and simmer until chickpeas are very soft, 1½-2 hrs. for dried chickpeas, or about 30 minutes for canned. Discard thyme sprig.
Purée chickpea mixture, adding water by ½ cupfuls if needed until smooth. Season with salt and pepper.
To make the broccoli, cook in a large pot of boiling salted water until crisp-tender about 4 minutes. Drain; rinse under cold water.
To serve soup, divide soup among 6 warmed bowls and garnish with broccoli, sour cream and thyme.

Tartare with Crisp Potato Chips

4 lunch servings or 8 appetizers

500 g bison, musk ox or beef fillet
3 tbsp. finely chopped onion
1 tbsp. capers, rinsed, drained and chopped
2 large pasteurized egg yolks

Potato chips:
1 large russet potato
oil for frying

Garnish:
¼ horseradish root, grated
1 red onion cut in rings
cress
lots of freshly ground black pepper

To make the tartare, place meat in freezer 30 minutes before using. It makes it easier to work with. Scrape meat with a very sharp knife, along the length of the muscle tissue, so you get fine, long segments of meat. Ensure there are no sinews in the finished tartare and place in a large bowl. Add onions, capers, egg yolks; stir until well combined. Cover and chill in the refrigerator for at least 30 minutes or until ready to use.

To make the potato chips, peel and slice potato very thinly. Keep them in cold water until ready to fry.

To fry, drain potato slices and pat them dry with a paper towel. Heat oil to 360°F and deep fry potato slices until golden brown and crispy, 2 to 3 minutes. Drain on paper towels and season with salt.

To serve, mold tartare into 4 patties and place on 4 plates. Push 3 or 4 potato chips into each patty. Garnish with grated horseradish, onion rings and cress. Sprinkle with lots of black pepper.

Variation: Instead of mixing the raw egg yolk in the tartare, place egg yolks in 4 half egg shells and position them in the middle of the tartare. Scatter small baby shrimps around the tartare as a replacement for homemade chips, horseradish and onion rings. Sprinkle with lots of black pepper.

Barley Soup with Kale, Spinach, and Dill

8 soup servings

4 cups water
8 cups (or more) vegetable broth
1 cup pearl barley
1 tsp. fine salt
2 tbsp. oil
3 finely chopped large onions
1 small head kale leaves, stemmed, coarsely chopped
5 oz. spinach leaves
4-5 chopped green onions
a handful chopped fresh dill
3 tbsp. chopped fresh mint
1-2 tbsp. fresh lemon juice
salt and freshly ground pepper
1-2 tbsp. rapeseed oil

To make the soup, bring 4 cups of water, 2 cups broth, barley and 1 tsp. salt to boil in a large pot. Reduce heat to medium low, cover and simmer until tender, about 40 minutes.

Meanwhile, heat 2 tbsp. oil in heavy medium skillet over medium-high heat. Add onions, sprinkle with salt and sauté until golden brown, stirring often, about 10 minutes. Add sautéed onions and remaining 6 cups of broth to pot with barley.

Add kale to soup. Simmer until greens are tender, about 15 minutes. Add spinach, green onions, dill and mint; simmer 5 minutes. Add 1-2 tbsp. lemon juice after taste, thinning with more broth, if desired. Season with salt and pepper.

To serve, divide soup among bowls. Drizzle with oil, and serve.

There are many types of kale to choose from. Dinosaur kale, also known as Lacinato, Tuscan, black kale, or cavolo nero, is most tender. Red Russian kale is slightly sweet. Denmark has mostly curly kale. The entire stem needs to be cut out of the leaf before cooking. Chopped stems can be eaten but need extra time to cook.

Cod with Roasted Beet Carpaccio, Bacon and Mustard Dressing

4 main course servings

1 lb. red beets
4 cod steaks, 1½ inch thick
½ cup white wine
1 bay leaf
6 peppercorns
4 hard boiled eggs
8 slices of bacon

Mustard sauce:
1 oz. fish mustard or Dijon mustard
½ cup white wine
½ cup fish broth
1 cups heavy cream
salt and freshly ground pepper

Garnish:
4 sprigs of chervil

To roast the beets, cut off green top but leave some stem and wash in cold water. Be sure not to break the skin, or juice will escape while cooking.
Preheat oven to 400°F. Place beets on baking sheet pan and bake for 30-40 minutes, until beets can be pierced easily with a toothpick. When cool enough to handle, peel them and cut them on a mandolin. Set aside.
To make the cod, bring wine, bay leaf, and peppercorns to boil in a large sauté pan or skillet. Place cod steaks in pan, cover and simmer 5 minutes. Remove pan from heat and let steaks remain in liquid an additional 5 minutes.
Fry bacon crisp on a warm skillet and transfer to paper towels.
Peel eggs and remove yolks. Chop whites of eggs. Set aside.
To make the mustard sauce, place mustard in a small casserole and when it is warm, add white wine. Add fish broth while stirring. Let sauce simmer 2-3 minutes. Add cream and cook until sauce thickens. Season with salt and pepper.
To serve, arrange beets in a circle on 4 warmed plates. Place a cod steak in the middle of beets. Crumble bacon and sprinkle around and over cod steaks. Push eggs yolks through a sieve and scatter them over the fish together with chopped egg whites. Top with a sprig of chervil. Serve with the mustard sauce.

Suggested accompaniment: fingerling potatoes.

Beer-Braised Veal Shanks and Root Vegetables

6 main course servings

4-6 (1 lb.) veal shanks, each cut into 1½-2 inch-thick pieces (osso buco)
salt and freshly ground pepper to taste
½ cup flour
1 tbsp. rapeseed oil
1 tbsp. butter
1½ cup dark beer
1 lemon, cut in wedges
1 bulb garlic, halved crosswise
a sprig of thyme
4 cups chicken stock
1½ lb. root vegetables such as carrots, celery, parsnips

Garnish:
4 sprigs of thyme

To make the veal shanks, preheat oven to 350°F. Season veal shanks with salt and pepper and lightly dust with flour. In a large sauté pan or skillet, brown meat in oil and butter. Add beer and bring to a boil.

Transfer shanks to ovenproof saucepan or Dutch oven just large enough to hold shanks in one layer. Place lemon, garlic and fresh thyme in pan and pour just enough bouillon to cover meat. Cut a circle of parchment that fits just inside pan and with a 1 inch hole in the center. Place paper over shanks to cover and braise in the oven 2½-3 hours or until shanks are very tender.

To make the vegetables, peel them and cut them in very thin slices. Place them on top of shanks and cook them 5-10 minutes.

To serve, place 1 veal shank on a warmed shallow plate, spoon vegetables and sauce over shanks. Garnish with a sprig of thyme.

Suggested accompaniment: mashed potatoes.

Striped Bass with Browned Hazelnut Butter and Celery Root, Kohlrabi and Apple Mash

8 main course servings

Mash:
2 lb. celery root, peeled, cut into ½ inch cubes
kosher salt
1 lb. kohlrabi, peeled, cut into 1 inch cubes
1 lb. russet potatoes, peeled, cut into 1 inch cubes
2 apples (½-3/4 lb.) peeled, cored, cut into 1 inch cubes
4 tbsp. butter
salt and freshly ground pepper

Fish:
8 4-5 oz. striped bass or branziono fillets with skin
salt and coarsely ground pepper
8 tbsp. butter
½ cup coarsely chopped toasted hazelnuts*

Garnish:
fresh chervil sprigs

To make the mash, bring a large pot of salted water to a boil and add celery root. Reduce heat to medium-low and simmer until tender, 10 minutes. Using a slotted spoon, transfer celery root to a large bowl. Return water to a boil; repeat with the kohlrabi, then potatoes, cooking each separately until tender, 15 minutes for kohlrabi and 10-20 minutes for potatoes; add to bowl with celery root.
To make the apples, bring apples and 2 tbsp. water to a boil in a small saucepan. Cover and cook over medium-high heat, stirring occasionally, until apples fall apart, 6-8 minutes, adding water by tablespoonfuls if dry.
Mash celery root, kohlrabi, potatoes, and apples with a potato masher. Stir in butter. Season with salt and pepper.
To make the fish, sprinkle fillet with salt and pepper. Melt 2 tbsp. butter in large skillet over medium-high heat. Add half of fillet, flesh side down. Cook until browned, 2-3 minutes. Turn fillets over; cook until opaque in center, 2-3 minutes. Transfer to plates; cook remaining fillets and transfer to plates. Cover to keep warm.
Add hazelnuts to same skillet over medium heat. Toast until golden, 1-2 minutes. Add remaining butter and cook until golden. Season with salt and pepper.
To serve, place fish on 8 plates and spoon hazelnuts over the fish. Place a scoop of mash next to the fish. Garnish with chervil sprigs.

* Leaving the skins on the toasted hazelnuts adds flavor and fiber.

Beer-Marinated Pork Tenderloin with Curly Kale Purée and Honey-Glazed Fingerlings

4-6 main course servings

2 pork tenderloins (1½-1¾ lbs. total) trimmed of fat
1 cup lager beer
2 tbsp. brown sugar
2 tbsp. apple cider vinegar
4 tbsp. rapeseed oil

Kale purée:
1½ lb. curly kale*
2 slices white bread, crust removed
1½ cups heavy cream
juice of 1 lemon
salt and freshly ground pepper
1 tsp. grated nutmeg

Glazed potatoes:
2 lbs. small fingerling potatoes, boiled and peeled
½ cup elderberry vinegar or another fruit vinegar
2 tbsp. honey

Garnish:
1 tsp. freshly grated nutmeg

To make the pork, place meat in a large resealable plastic bag. Whisk beer, brown sugar and vinegar in a small bowl; pour into bag with pork and seal. Chill, turning occasionally, for at least 4 and up to 24 hours.
Preheat the oven to 400°F. Heat oil in a large ovenproof skillet over medium-high heat. Remove pork from marinade, allowing any excess to drip off. Cook pork, turning, until browned on all sides 8-10 minutes.
Transfer skillet to oven and roast until a thermometer inserted into the thickest part of pork registers 140°F, 10-15 minutes. Transfer to a plate and let rest for at least 10 minutes.
To make the kale puree, cook kale 10 min. in lightly salted water. Strain kale and chop together with bread. Reduce cream by half in a heavy bottomed saucepan, add kale and bread and cook a few minutes. Season with salt, pepper, lemon juice and grated nutmeg.
To make honey glazed fingerlings, cook vinegar and honey in a skillet until it becomes syrupy. Add the fingerlings, brown them, turning constantly.
To serve, slice pork and serve with kale puree and fingerling potatoes. Sprinkle with grated nutmeg.

* Denmark has mostly curly kale. The entire stem needs to be cut out of the leaf before cooking. Chopped stems can be eaten but need extra time to cook.

Reindeer Medallions with Chanterelle and Spinach

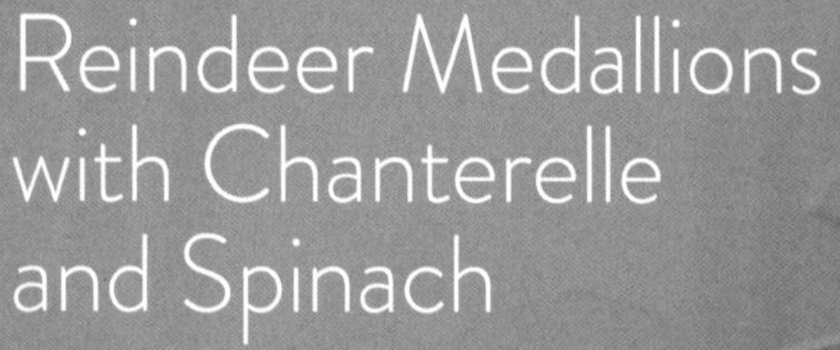

6 main course servings

Sauce:
1 tbsp. butter
1 finely chopped shallot
2 juniper berries
1 sprig of thyme
½ cup white wine
½ cup pear juice
½ cup blackcurrant juice
2 cups venison stock (see page 107) or store bought veal stock
1 tbsp. apple cider vinegar
3 oz. butter

Spinach:
16 oz. spinach
5 tbsp. butter

Venison:
2-2½ lbs. venison fillet, sliced in 12 equal parts
2 oz. butter

Chanterelle:
3 oz. chanterelle
1 tbsp. butter

Garnish:
Sprigs of thyme

To make the sauce, melt the butter in a skillet over medium heat, add shallot, thyme and juniper berries and sauté until golden. Add wine, pear and blackcurrant juice and cook until reduced by half. Add venison stock, apple cider vinegar and cook until reduced by half. Whip butter in a little at a time until it is all incorporated. Set the sauce aside.

To make the venison, sauté tournedos 2 minutes on each side. Just before serving, sauté chanterelle on a warm pan in butter. Using the same skillet, sauté spinach 1-2 minutes.

To serve, place tournedos on 6 warmed plates. Place spinach and chanterelle next to them. Heat sauce carefully and spoon over the tournedos and onto the plate. Garnish with thyme.

Suggested accompaniment: fingerling potatoes.

Venison stock:

This stock can be made a few days ahead of time.

bones cut* into 2 inch pieces
1 onion, coarsely chopped
1 carrot, coarsely chopped
¼ celery root, peeled and cut into 1 inch pieces
3 bay leaves
2 tsp. black peppercorns
3 fresh thyme sprigs
enough water to cover bones

Preheat oven to 400°F.

To make the venison stock, put bones in a large roasting pan together with onion, carrot, celery and roast until golden brown, about 30 minutes. Transfer bones and herbs to a large stockpot. Fill pot with enough cold water to just cover the bones. Bring to a boil and skim off any foam that develops.

Add remaining ingredients; bring back to a boil, then decrease the heat to simmer. Cook at least 2 hours and up to 12 hours. Keep adding hot water to maintain water level, which you will need to do 5-6 times if you cook for 12 hours.

Strain through a fine-mesh sieve into a smaller pot and cook over high heat until reduced to about 5-6 cups, about 1 hour.

* If it is not possible to cut the bones yourself, ask the butcher to cut them for you.

Oxtails with Crushed potatoes

6 main course servings

5 tbsp. vegetable oil, divided
4 lbs. oxtails or beef shanks
salt and freshly ground pepper
3 large shallots, coarsely chopped
2 medium carrots, peeled, coarsely chopped
4 garlic cloves, chopped
2 sprigs of thyme
1 tsp. juniper berries
2 cups dry red wine
1½ quart veal stock
water
salt and freshly ground pepper
2 tbsp. butter

Crushed potatoes:
2 lbs. baking potatoes
3 oz. butter
3 oz. Danish cheese Vesterhavsost* or Havarti
1 bunch finely chopped parsley

To make the oxtails, heat 1 tbsp. oil in a large heavy pot over medium-high heat. Season oxtails with salt and pepper. Working in batches, cook until browned on all sides, adding 1 tbsp. oil between each batch, 10-15 minutes per batch; transfer to a plate.
Add remaining oil to same pot. Add shallots, carrots, garlic, thyme sprigs, juniper berries. Cook, stirring occasionally, until golden brown, 8-10 minutes. Add wine and cook until reduced by half. Add veal stock; return oxtails to pot. Add enough water so the oxtails are just covered. Bring to a boil; reduce heat, cover and simmer, stirring occasionally, until meat is fork-tender, 2½-3 hours. Transfer oxtails to a plate. Strain stock through a fine-mesh sieve into a bowl (discard solids). Return stock to pot and reduce by half. Whip butter in and season with salt and pepper.
To make the crushed potatoes, bake potatoes 1 hour in a 400°F warm oven. Once cool, peel the skins off. Using an electric mixer, crush potatoes. Add butter and sprinkle with cheese.
To serve, arrange oxtails on a large platter, pour a little sauce over and pass the rest of the sauce at the table. Place potatoes in a bowl and sprinkle with parsley.

*Danish Vesterhavsost can be replaced with parmesan.

Braised Pork Cheeks in Dark Beer and Apple Cider with Farro

4 main course servings

Gastrique*:
1½ cup dark brown sugar
1 cup apple cider vinegar

Pork cheeks:
12 pork cheeks, trimmed for fat and sinew
½ head of celery root, peeled and cut in smaller pieces
2 onions cut in smaller pieces
2 apples, peeled, quartered, cored
2 cups apple cider
1 bottle strong, dark beer
2 oz. butter

Farro with wild mushrooms and herbs:
1 cup semi-pearled farro
3 cups water
kosher salt
1 tbsp. corn oil
4 oz. assorted fresh mushrooms (such as chanterelle, porcini and crimini) cut in 1 inch pieces
freshly ground black pepper
1 cup chicken broth
2 tbsp. butter
1 tbsp. chopped flat-leaf parsley
1 tbsp. chopped fresh chives
1 tbsp. chopped fresh thyme

*1 tbsp. of honey can be used instead of Gastrique.

To make the gastrique, boil sugar and vinegar in a large saucepan until reduced to ½ cup, about 30 minutes. Set gastrique aside.
To make the pork cheeks, preheat oven to 400°F. Melt 2 oz. of butter in a large ovenproof skillet with a tight fitting lid over medium-high heat. Brown pork cheeks, turning, until browned on all sides, 8-10 minutes.
Arrange celery root, onions and apples around the pork. Add cider and beer. Bring to a boil over high heat, cover and transfer to oven. Braise pork cheeks 1½-2 hours until a knife slides easily through meat.
Transfer meat from braising liquid and keep it warm. Strain braising liquid through a fine-mesh sieve into a saucepan; discard fat. Bring to a boil over high heat. Boil sauce until reduced to 1 cup, about 10 minutes. Add gastrique or honey, and season to taste with salt and pepper. Add butter gradually, stirring slowly (do not whisk) until it is all absorbed.
To make the farro, cook farro in boiling salted water until tender, about 20 minutes. Drain, let cool and set aside. Heat the oil in a large skillet over medium-high heat. Add mushrooms, cook, turning once, until crisp and cooked through, 4-5 minutes. Transfer to a plate and season with salt and pepper.
Bring broth to a simmer in a medium saucepan over medium heat. Add farro and cook, stirring often, until heated through. Season the farro with salt and pepper. Add butter and stir to combine and create a creamy texture. Add mushrooms, parsley, chives and thyme and stir to an even blend.
To serve, drizzle the pork cheeks with the sauce. Serve remaining sauce alongside. Serve with farro with wild mushrooms and herbs.

Suggested accompaniment: steamed green beans.

Farro with Bacon, Leeks and Poached Eggs

6 main course servings

5 cups chicken broth
6 slices thick cut bacon, cut crosswise into ½ inch pieces
1 large or two small leeks, white and pale green parts only, chopped coarsely
1½ cup farro
¾ cup dry white wine
3 tbsp. finely chopped fresh large leafed parsley
1 tbsp. butter
salt and freshly ground pepper

Poached eggs:
6 large eggs
water
salt

Garnish:
chopped parsley, chopped leeks

To make the farro, bring broth to a simmer in medium saucepan; cover to keep warm. Heat a large skillet over medium heat. Add bacon and cook until crisp, stirring occasionally. Using slotted spoon, transfer bacon to paper towels to drain. Add leeks to drippings in pan; cook until soft but not brown, stirring often, 4-5 minutes. Transfer 2 generous tablespoonfuls leeks to a small bowl; reserve for garnish. Add farro to pan; stir 1-2 minutes. Add wine; stir until absorbed, about 2 minutes. Add ½ cup warm broth to skillet; stir until broth is absorbed. Repeat adding broth and stirring until farro is tender but still firm to bite and sauce is creamy, about 20-25 minutes. Add bacon, parsley and butter. Season to taste with salt and pepper.

To make the eggs, bring a large skillet of water just to a simmer over medium-low heat. Sprinkle water with salt. Working with 1 egg at a time, crack into small bowl and slide egg into simmering water. Cook eggs until whites are cooked but yolks are still runny, 3 to 4 minutes. Using slotted spoon, carefully transfer poached eggs to medium bowl filled with ice water.

To serve, divide farro among 6 bowls. Top with poached egg. Sprinkle with salt and pepper. Sprinkle with parsley leaves and reserved leeks.

Beef Tenderloin Stew

4 main course servings

8 tbsp. butter
2 10 oz. beef fillets, cut into ½ x ½ inch strips
2 onions cut into wedges
16 oz. wild mushrooms, divided, one portion sliced*
½ cup snaps/aquavit**
2 cups heavy cream
salt and freshly ground pepper

Garnish:
4 tbsp. sour cream
1 portion wild mushrooms (see top of the page)

To make the stew, melt 6 tbsp. butter in a large skillet over medium-high heat. Add fillet strips and sauté briefly on all sides until browned. Transfer to a strainer placed over a bowl and allow beef to drain. Reserve beef and its juices separately.

Melt remaining butter in same skillet over medium-high heat. Add onions and half of mushrooms and cook, stirring until the onion is wilted. Add snaps and scrape up any browned bits from bottom of skillet. Add reserved meat juices and cream and cook, stirring until sauce is reduced and thickened, 10 to 15 minutes. Season with salt and pepper. Add beef strips to the sauce and heat through.

To serve, transfer stew to a warmed platter and garnish with the remaining raw mushrooms and sour cream.

* The wild mushrooms must be fresh, if not, sauté them in the stew.

** Snaps, also known as aquavit, is a traditional flavored sprit and is a specialty of Denmark.

Horseradish-Glazed Brisket with Root Vegetable Mash

8 main course servings

Brine:
5 oz. coarse kosher salt
1½ oz. sugar
2 bay leaves
1 tsp. whole black peppercorns
2-3 sprigs of parsley
1 cup celery leaves
2-3 sprigs of thyme
1 3½-3¾ lb. flat-cut beef brisket

Braising liquid:
water
1 onion
1 carrot
1 leek
1 sprig of thyme

Glaze:
1 tbsp. prepared horseradish
1 tbsp. Dijon mustard
1 tbsp. packed brown sugar
salt and freshly ground pepper

Vegetable Mash:
1 large celery root, peeled, cut in 1-1½ inch cubes
2 large rutabaga, peeled, cut in 1 inch cubes
1 lb. potatoes, peeled, cut in 1½ inch cubes
3 oz. butter
salt and freshly ground pepper

To make the brisket, bring 1 cup of water to boil with salt and sugar. Place brisket in a heavy wide pot. Add salt/sugar mixture, bay leaves, peppercorns, parsley, celery leaves, sprigs of thyme and enough water to cover meat. Place a small plate on top of brisket in order to keep meat in the brine. Set brisket in the brine in the refrigerator or someplace cold. The meat should stay in the brine 2 days. On the third day, take brisket up and run it under cold water. Discard brine and place meat in pot, add enough water to cover meat. Bring to simmer over medium heat. Skim any impurities that rise to the surface. Reduce heat and add onion, carrot, leek and thyme. Cover; simmer until meat is fork-tender, about 2 hours. Save the cooking liquid.

Preheat oven to 375°F.

Transfer the meat to a 15x10x2 inch glass baking dish.

To make the horseradish glaze, whisk the horseradish, mustard and sugar together and brush over the meat. Sprinkle with salt and pepper. Roast meat until brown and heated through, 20 minutes.

To make the mash, bring cooking liquid to boil; add the celery root, rutabaga and potatoes. Reduce heat to medium and cook uncovered until vegetables are tender, about 45 minutes. Drain vegetables, reserving 1½ cup cooking liquid. Return vegetables to pot and stir over low heat 1 minute to dry. Mash vegetables with potato masher to a coarse puree. Add 1 tbsp. of cooking liquid at a time until mash has the right consistence. Mash in butter. Season to taste with salt and pepper.

To serve, transfer meat to work surface. Thinly slice across grain. Place on platter. Drizzle reserved cooking liquid around. Serve with vegetable mash and additional horseradish sauce.

Suggested accompaniment: steamed Brussels sprouts.

Small Buttermilk Cakes with Sour Milk Compote and Aquavit Cherries

12 dessert servings

Buttermilk cakes:
1¼ cup unsalted butter
2 cups flour
1 tsp. baking soda
1 tsp. salt
1 cup sugar
2 large eggs
1 cup buttermilk

Sour milk compote:
2 cups whole milk
1 cup sugar
2 cups crème fraiche

Cherries:
1 cup dried tart cherries
1 cup snaps/aquavit*
½ cup sugar

Special equipment:
12 individual small forms

Preheat oven to 350°F.

To make the cakes, butter and flour the forms. Whisk baking soda, salt, and 2 cups flour in a medium bowl; set aside.

In another bowl, beat sugar and butter until light and fluffy. Add eggs one at a time, beating to blend between additions and scraping down sides of bowl. Add dry ingredients a little at a time alternating with buttermilk. Pour batter into prepared forms. Bake until cakes are golden and a tester inserted into the center comes out clean, 20-25 minutes. Cool and turn cakes out.

To make sour milk compote, bring milk and sugar to a boil in a small saucepan over medium heat, stirring to dissolve sugar; reduce heat and simmer gently, whisking occasionally, until mixture is reduced to ½ cup. Transfer to a small bowl; let cool. Whisk in crème fraiche when milk has thickened, cover and chill.

To make the cherries, bring cherries, aquavit, sugar and 1 cup water to a boil in a saucepan; reduce heat and simmer until liquid is syrupy, 6-8 minutes. Let cool.

To serve, spoon a dollop of compote on 12 plates and place a cake on top. Top with cherries.

* Snaps, also known as aquavit, is a traditional flavored sprit and is a specialty of Denmark.

Bread and beer porridge is normally a breakfast dish and is made with dry Danish rye bread and non-alcoholic beer. Now it is a dessert dish and can be made with both white and dark chocolate, sugar, orange juice and served with heavy cream, caramel ice cream, vanilla ice cream, nuts, oats and much more.

Bread and Beer Porridge with Chocolate and Orange-Nut Crunch

6 dessert servings

1 lb., several days old, dark rye bread, (see page 33)
cut into ½ inch cubes
1 dark beer
½ cup sugar
1 oz. grated chocolate

Garnish:
1 tbsp. butter
½ tbsp. sugar
2 oz. hazelnuts, slightly crushed
1 orange peel without the white part, cut into thin strips
Vanilla ice cream

To make the porridge, soak bread cubes in beer 2 hours or overnight. Cook bread cubes with beer, sugar and chocolate 10 minutes. Blend porridge and let cool.

To make the orange-nut crunch, melt butter in a skillet. Add sugar, nuts and orange strips and cook until golden brown and crisp. Transfer to paper towel to drain.

To serve, divide porridge among 6-8 warmed shallow bowls, and spoon a large tablespoon of ice cream over porridge and sprinkle with orange-nut crunch.

Christmas Pudding with Hot Cherry Sauce

6 dessert servings

1¾ pint whole milk
3 oz. short-grained rice
½ tsp. salt
1 tsp. pure vanilla extract
2 oz. blanched, coarsely chopped almonds
1½ cup heavy cream, whipped
1 whole almond (optional)

Cherry sauce:
1 lb. canned stoned cherries in their syrup
1½ tsp. cornstarch

To make the pudding, bring milk to a boil in a heavy-bottomed pot. Add rice gradually, stirring constantly. Cook mixture over low heat for 50 minutes. Be careful not to let the rice burn. Remove pot from heat and stir in salt.
When rice-mixture is cold, stir in vanilla extract and chopped almonds. Fold in whipped cream. Refrigerate before serving.
To make the cherry sauce, place cherries and their syrup in a saucepan and bring to boil. Dissolve cornstarch in a little water. Pour into the boiling hot liquid, stirring constantly.
Serve the hot cherry sauce immediately with the cold rice pudding.

This is the traditional Christmas Eve dessert in Denmark. One blanched whole almond is hidden in the pudding just before serving. All the guests at the table serve themselves with a small or large serving of the pudding depending on how much they want to win the "Almond present". Whoever gets the hidden almond wins a special gift. It is a contest that everyone wants to win. The person who has the almond will try to hide the almond, making everyone keep eating even after they are full. So, be sure to make plenty of Christmas pudding.

Index of Recipes

Lynn Andersen: Modern Danish Cooking
Photos: Jann Stokking

ISBN 978-87-17-04364-0

Editor: Lise Heilesen
Printed at Clemenstrykkeriet A/S, Hinnerup, DK
Graphic design: Louise Zyskind

Set in Brandon Grotesque

Printed in Denmark 2014

Nyt Nordisk Forlag Arnold Busck A/S
Pilestræde 52, 3
1112 København K.
nnf@nytnordiskforlag.dk · www.nytnordiskforlag.dk

Follow Lynn Andersen on her blog:
moderndanishcooking.com